The Second Mile

THE SECOND MILE

Edited by

Sue Davidson

CONTEMPORARY

APPROACHES

IN   COUNSELING

YOUNG WOMEN

NEW DIRECTIONS FOR YOUNG WOMEN
TUCSON, ARIZONA

Library of Congress Cataloging in Publication Data

Main entry under title:

The Second mile.

    Bibliography: p.
    1. Adolescent girls—United States—Social conditions—Addresses,
essays, lectures. 2. Young women—United States—Social conditions—
Addresses, essays, lectures. 3. Counseling—United States—Addresses,
essays, lectures. I. Davidson, Sue, 1925– . II. New Directions for Young
Women, inc.
HQ798.S42 1983   362.7'96   83-19389
ISBN 0-9608696-2-X

Publication of this book was made possible by a grant from the
Lilly Endowment, Inc., Indianapolis, Indiana. Points of view are those
of the authors and do not necessarily represent the views of the Lilly
Endowment.

Book design: Rachel da Silva and Dan Zucker

This book was typeset by Franklin Press and printed by
Workshop Printers, both of Seattle, Washington.

Table of Contents

Introduction

"The world," comments twelve-year-old Frankie Addams, in *The Member of the Wedding,* "is certainly a sudden place." Adolescence is perplexing, and the world has become a more sudden place than the one experienced by Frankie in the early 1940s. In the intervening years, technological and cultural change have taken place at ever-increasing speeds. So rapid are the changes, that in the very midst of identifying a novel cultural development, we see it replaced by another. To give but one example relevant to youth: at the same time that social commentators were voicing concern at the lethargy of the first generation of television-reared children, that same generation was gathering the initiative for a mass movement of running away from home. Although hindsight offers some explanations of that unexpected episode, it is difficult to predict patterns of youth behavior which may be shaping as these lines are written.

In spite of rapid change, however, many of the pressing social problems faced by adolescents today are not new. What is new is their large-scale application to a youthful, rather than an adult, population. Prostitution, often called the world's oldest profession, has only relatively recently employed children in staggering numbers in the United States. Even the estimates of one million or more juveniles involved in prostitution by 1978 represented an increase of 428.2 percent over the previous decade.[1] According to available data, twice as many girls as boys are prostitutes.[2] Noncommercial sexual activity on the part of adolescents, particularly that of females, has also been rising sharply, with initiation of girls occurring at younger ages in the past ten years. It is also the younger adolescent women who account for the steepest increases in teenage pregnancy, abortion, and birth rates. Between 1961–

1981, the birth rate among fourteen-to-seventeen year old women increased 75 percent; births to all teenage women represent nearly 20 percent of total U.S. births.[3] With limited skills and education, these young mothers are likely to join the pool of female-headed households of which 70 percent live in poverty.[4] Sixty-one percent of AFDC recipients are women who bore their first child in their teens.[5]

The need to cope prematurely with adult experience falls more heavily upon female than upon male adolescents. Females are more frequently victimized by such experience, and their life options are more narrow. Yet, even in the alarm over the emerging problems of youth—drugs and alcohol, venereal disease, unemployment, depression, suicide, violence, incarceration—the special problems and conditions faced by teenage females have been largely overlooked.

The writings brought together in this volume report on the work of those who have taken seriously the needs of today's young women, particularly young women who suffer social and economic disadvantages. It is doubtful that any of these articles could have been written ten years ago; indeed, the earliest work reported here was undertaken in the mid-1970s. Although varying degrees of attention had previously been given to the special populations which are the focus of some of these articles—for example, racial and sexual minorities and the disabled—the unique condition of their youthful female members was generally not recognized. And while unwed motherhood and prostitution have long been regarded as social problems, it was the threateningly open sexuality of the females, not their exploitation, that was the usual object of concern.[6] Finally, before the rise of the contemporary women's movement, matters such as rape, abortion, and battering were viewed as individual private problems. There were no special counseling programs for battered or raped women, no network of legal and medical services, until the crisis centers established by women exposed the proportions of these problems. As to the adolescent females whose development is profoundly affected by such traumatic experiences, they remain, even today, all but invisible in programs for youth and in the literature available to those who work with youth.

The most desperate need of many young women is to find the economic means of survival. While females today are still being socialized to believe that their security lies in marriage and mother-hood, surveys of teenage mothers indicate that approximately 90 percent receive no financial aid from the fathers of their children.[7] Few employment programs answer to the unique needs of these young women, many of whom also face racial discrimination in their search for jobs. In "Learning the Ropes," we see that it is possible to strengthen these young mothers' chances in the job market. In the program described here, sessions which improve communication abilities, identify already-acquired skills, deal sen-sibly with stress, teach about the world of work and the value of as-sertiveness, were specifically designed for inner city teenage mothers, and their effects tested. Anchored in a pragmatic ap-proach, the training achieved positive results, enabling the young women to take a crucial step toward self-sufficiency.

"Si Necesita Ayuda, Llame . . ." ("If You Need Help, Call . . .") provides a description of the work of the East Los Angeles Rape Hotline, an organization which gives crisis aid and counseling to a generally neglected group: Latinas. This selection offers an orien-tation to care which will be revealing even to those experienced with rape counseling, in its analysis of the complex cultural factors that influence both the Latina rape survivor and her counselors. Hotline workers stress the need not only for Spanish-speaking services, but for a thoroughly bicultural approach to the Latina in crisis, informed by awareness of the enormous diversity of the Latino community. Although the Chicana feminists who created the Hotline did not foresee it, care of the young Latina developed into a priority, simply because women in their teens and early twenties were the most numerous clientele. The insights gleaned from the practice of this pioneering organization can serve as a consciousness-raiser to all who provide assistance to young Latinas and their families.

The initial purpose of New Directions for Young Women, founded in Tucson, Arizona, in 1976, was to offer alternatives to incarceration for young women affected by the juvenile justice sys-tem. Its mission soon broadened, by necessity, to encompass the range of problems and populations treated in the present volume. The title article, *The Second Mile,* describes the work of the agency, which combines direct services with efforts to induce institutional change. Like the East Los Angeles Rape Hotline, New Directions grew out of the women's movement and incorporates feminist principles in its counseling approach. The dynamic of this approach emerges in narrative and interviews which illustrate typical circumstances faced by New Directions clients: unintended pregnancy, single motherhood, homelessness, unemployment, family violence, sexual abuse, school dropout. Through informational programs and innovative groups, New Directions offers clients the tools they need for dealing with their experience and environment. Counselors help clients to define the choices open to them; act as their advocates with the systems and individuals bearing most directly on their lives; and serve them as a continuing reservoir of emotional support.

The group counseling model presented in *Teenage Street Women* is based on needs identified by numerous adolescent prostitutes, contacted in the course of a sensitive study, as well as on clinical practice and field observations. All exercises in this model are linked to the central goal of improving the self-concept of teenage street women. Other observers have noted the drop in self-esteem which typically occurs in both males and females at the onset of biological maturity. Most counseling approaches, however, turn a blind eye to the demeaning messages adolescent women receive from society, which work to undermine their self-respect. Unlike these, the model presented here consciously seeks to overcome negative stereotypes of women, particularly the emphasis on women as sex objects which has become inescapable in the mass media. The model also directs attention to basic sex and health education and to building capacities for "straight world" problem-solving, areas of special significance for young street women.

Few subjects are more fraught with controversy in our society than that of sexual identity. The very recent social recognition of non-heterosexuality has not led to social acceptance; and social service agencies have responded inadequately, when they have responded at all, to the needs of adolescent lesbians and gays. *More Open Doors* describes the consequences of current negative attitudes for the young people affected. Family conflict and breakdown are common, whether the reaction is one of denial, pressure on the adolescent to change and become "normal," anger, or rejection. Even without outright rejection, lack of family and social support during the critical teen years has repercussions which may range in severity from substance abuse and running away to suicide. *More Open Doors* points to the urgent need for education which addresses bias and misconceptions in the counseling of sexual minority youth, and suggests organizing strategies aimed at increasing the resources available to this under-served population.

Addictive Love and Abuse reports on what is probably the first course of study on battering ever offered to adolescent women. Although some surveys suggest that many abusive relationships begin in adolescence, shelters and informational/counseling programs serve adult women almost exclusively. Even were shelters not prohibited, as some are, from taking in adolescent women, teenagers are difficult to reach. The participants in the program described here attended the sessions as an elective course, taught in an alternative high school setting. The sessions were held with two groups, one predominantly white, the other predominantly black; the latter was composed of pregnant and parent teenagers. Through a series of imaginative exercises, the young women were drawn into eager participation, finding new ways to examine their experience, and at the same time contributing valuable insights and information about abusive teen relationships. While the major goals of the course were realized, the author/course leader notes ideas for alterations, additions, and further development suggested by the experimental course.

Attitudes toward disabled people have historically been characterized by an ignorance and prejudice which results in exclusion of the disabled from the social mainstream and in extreme economic hardship. In the past decade, under the pressure of a movement by and for disabled people, a re-examination of their situation, needs, and capacities for work and independent living has begun; but services designed for this population are still in a primitive stage of development. *Access to the Future* documents the double discrimination visited upon disabled females—tripled if they are women of color—and analyzes sex bias and stereotyping as these affect services for disabled female youth. Major issues in the counseling of disabled young women are illumined—role models, education, independence, work, and interpersonal relationships. Bringing to their subject a background gained in projects which are pathbreaking in their focus on disabled female youth, the authors outline sound and positive strategies for change.

In the pages that follow, readers will find a wealth of specific suggestions for improved counseling of today's young women. This volume, however, is not simply a "how to" manual. The central message of these selection, taken together, is that effective counseling of the youth described here depends upon an understanding of the position of women in society, both traditionally and as it is being shaped by current forces. Such an understanding leads not only to more enlightened counseling of individual young women, but to pressures for necessary changes in the systems which affect the welfare of all young women. The work described in this volume represents an important contribution to the beginning of that process.

Sue Davidson

NOTES

1.   Debra Boyer and Jennifer James, "Easy Money: Adolescent Involvement in Prostitution," in *Justice for Young Women: Close-up on Critical Issues*, edited by Sue Davidson (Tucson, Ariz.: New Directions for Young Women, 1982), p. 77. The authors cite F.B.I. *Uniform Crime Reports*, 1978. Other surveys estimate that 1.2 million children under sixteen are involved annually in prostitution, pornography, or both. See Florence Rush, "Child Pornography", in *Take Back the Night*, edited by Laura Lederer (New York: Bantam Books, 1982), p. 70.

2.   "Juvenile Prostitution: A Federal Strategy for Combatting Its Causes and Consequences," submitted to the Youth Development Bureau, Office of Human Development, H.E.W., 1978.

3.   Lenore Hershey, "Girls Are People," paper presented to national meeting of Girls Clubs of America, Oct. 28, 1981, p. 3; and Beatrix A. Hamburg, M.D., "Developmental Issues in School-Age Pregnancy," paper presented at the International Conference on Aspects of Psychiatric Problems of Childhood and Adolescence, Paris, November 14–16, 1979, p. 4.

4.   Coalition on Women and the Budget, *Inequality of Sacrifice: The Impact of the Reagan Budget on Women* (Washington, D.C., March 16, 1983), p. 2.

5. Hamburg, p. 21.

6. Meda Chesney-Lind, "Judicial Paternalism and the Female Status Offender: Training Women to Know Their Place," *Crime and Delinquency*, April 1977, pp. 121–130.

7. The Alan Guttmacher Institute, *Teenage Pregnancy: The Problem That Hasn't Gone Away* (New York, 1981), p. 31.

The Second Mile

Learning the Ropes:
Job-seeking Skills for
Teenage Mothers

Lewayne D. Gilchrist, Deborah Lodish,
Susan Staab, and Steven Paul Schinke

Teenagers are the largest group of unemployed persons in the United States.[1] Eighteen percent of all female teenage students who want to work are unemployed; a sadly larger 24.6 percent of their same-age counterparts who quit school are unemployed. Overall, adolescents from racial and ethnic minority groups are unemployed at higher rates than any other group. Black adolescent students have an out-of-work rate of 44.8 percent.[2] The overall unemployment rate for young minority women is 45.5 percent.[3] Forty-four percent of black adolescents who leave school—often to take a job—are unemployed.[4] For teenage women forced to terminate their educations because of pregnancy, employment prospects are bleaker still. One recent large-scale study revealed that 91 percent of a sample of women giving birth at ages fifteen through nineteen had neither full- nor part-time employment nineteen months after delivery.[5] Teenage mothers are over twice as likely to fall below federal poverty lines as women who became mothers at twenty or older.[6] Many young single mothers are members of minority races and face the problem of racism in the job

The authors are grateful to the Aetna Life and Casualty Company and to Mary Ann Liebert of Medina Children's Services, Seattle, for their generous support of this work. The program would not have been developed without the expertise of Josie Solseng Maxwell, Betty J. Blythe, and Richard P. Barth. Anna P. Bolstad contributed significantly to the production of this report.

1

market. Research indicates that when black and white high-school graduates compete for the same jobs, white graduates are more likely to be hired even though black graduates may be more qualified.[7] In sum, lack of education, lack of marketable skills, lack of experience, and employers' discriminatory attitudes combine to significantly reduce young mothers' chances for self-sufficiency through employment. One result of this lack of employment is that 55 percent of teenage mothers receive public assistance and half of all payments for aid to families with dependent children go to women who bore children in adolescence.[8]

Few if any people who are dependent upon the public welfare system are satisfied with their welfare status.[9] More than 93 percent of teenage mothers choose to keep their children, and these young women are particularly dependent on public welfare for support.[10] Yet, in one study, over 95 percent of young mothers stated that they far prefer work to welfare.[11] How can human service professionals help young mothers get the work they want? One step toward an answer involves learning what constitutes effective job-getting behavior and then teaching this behavior to young mothers. Such an approach would equip practitioners with a powerful means for increasing young mothers' employment prospects.

The work outlined in this paper focused on assessing and analyzing skills necessary for young mothers to find and get jobs and on empirically testing a training program for teaching teenage mothers these crucial skills. As the Results section shows, the skills-training program strengthened young mothers' chances of obtaining entry level jobs. The work presented here represents a fruitful collaboration between a group of university-based researchers and a community agency committed to high quality service to inner-city, racial minority adolescent mothers. We hope this work will provide practitioners in a variety of settings with efficient guidelines for teaching young women to locate viable job opportunities, to present themselves effectively to prospective employers, and to cope with the stresses of employment once they get a job. Participants were forty-six mothers or mothers-to-be ranging in age from thirteen to nineteen years. Forty of these young mothers were black, three were white, two were Hispanic, and one was a Native American. The average age of participants' children was 8.29 months. Twelve participants were pregnant at the time of the study.

Specifically, the study compiled a comprehensive series of skills that young mothers must master to find and get a job. We began by interviewing managers or assistant managers of fast food establishments and other local businesses that hire teenagers. We asked these managers to describe as explicitly as possible their hiring practices and the characteristics and behavior that they liked and disliked in the job applicants they frequently screened. Combining data from these employer interviews with research literature on effective job getting[12] and eliminating overlapping items yielded a useful pool of tasks that teenage women need to manage successfully in order to be competitive with other candidates. These tasks included getting job leads from friends and other sources, managing anxiety related to risking possible rejection, telephoning to get information about potential jobs and to set up an interview, arranging transportation and daycare if necessary, filling out written job applications completely and accurately, presenting themselves positively and enthusiastically in a hiring interview, and following up to find out the status of their application.

We then gave this list of job-related tasks to a group of young mothers and asked them to indicate how they would handle each of the tasks and their past experiences with job applications and interviews. Young mothers' general attitudes toward employment were rated by tabulating how much they agreed or disagreed with such statements as: "If I heard someone talking about an interesting job opening, I'd be reluctant to ask for more information unless I knew the person"; "I'd downplay my qualifications so that an employer won't think I'm more qualified than I really am"; "If someone told me that a potential manager was too busy to see me, I would stop trying to contact that employer"; "Getting the job I want is largely a matter of luck."[13] Comparing information from employers with the job habits and attitudes described by young mothers yielded interesting discrepancies. In sum, although more than 60 percent of the young mothers had held at least one paying job, many of them seemed not to understand the hiring process, and had trouble anticipating employers' needs or concerns. Virtually none of them had developed job-search strategies to increase their knowledge of viable job openings. Young mothers in the skills-analysis phase of our work consistently demonstrated that they did not know how to summarize their past experience in positive terms, and did not see how the skills they demonstrated in other jobs applied to the job they were seeking.

Employers in our study indicated a preference for youth who demonstrated energy, enthusiasm, and a self-confident belief that they might get the job and perform well in it. Young mothers, on the other hand, experienced considerable difficulty in making positive comments about themselves. They were consistently self-deprecating or silent regarding even their most impressive qualifications. This finding is in keeping with other studies that consistently find minority youths—and young women, in particular—"characterized by a passive presentation of self."[14] Our young mothers were no exception. Their lack of self-assertion and their passivity during the job application process came across as lack of energy, lack of enthusiasm, and lack of interest in the job. Lack of skill in managing stress appeared to impede young mothers' job search and job application activities. Stress researchers have consistently reported differences between women's and men's styles of coping with challenging or distressing situations.[15] Men, in general, tend to select direct, goal-oriented actions when faced with a task, challenge, or problem. Women, on the other hand, tend to select less direct approaches, and often focus coping efforts on controlling their negative feelings, with no increases in goal-oriented behavior. Our sample of young mothers behaved consistently with this model. They described the job search and application process as stressful, and coped with this discomfort through avoidance techniques—postponing interviews, phone calls, and "getting into the job thing" as long as possible.

Specific examples of young mothers' job-finding strategies flesh out these general conclusions. Young mothers as a group thought it best to drop in on businesses to apply for jobs at lunch time or just before dinner (i.e., times that were convenient for themselves). These times were singled out by all managers, and particularly those in fast food establishments, as especially hectic or inappropriate, and as placing job applicants at a distinct disadvantage. Managers, on the whole, liked to screen applicants through telephone calls and to set up interviews in this manner. Young mothers almost unanimously chose not to telephone, because they felt uncomfortable in doing so. Managers liked applicants who forthrightly stated their positive qualities. Almost all young mothers saw this response as inappropriate "bragging." Over a third of the young mothers believed that the best response to the application question, "Why do you want this job?" was "My father (or someone else) told me I needed a job." The managers were unanimous in their negative reaction to this job-seeking rationale, and far preferred responses indicating independent personal motivation—for example, "I need the money," or "I want experience." Inexperienced young mothers believed that they would be closely questioned about their child. Some thought the best response was a long defensive explanation about how well the child was being raised. Others, believing that their parenthood biased employers against them, thought it best to deny that they had any dependents. Managers, on the other hand, never asked directly about dependents. The few who solicited information about "anything that would affect what hours you work" reported liking direct (and true) responses best.

Program Planning

On the basis of the preprogram needs assessment, we made several decisions regarding required components of a responsive job skills training program for young mothers. Skills analysis revealed that the young women needed a clear view of the whole job application process. They needed to anticipate realistically the priorities and concerns of employers. They needed techniques for managing stress and for assertively presenting their positive qualities and past experiences, in order to appear more confident and qualified in face-to-face interviews and in telephone contacts with prospective employers. On the basis of this analysis, we developed a concentrated skills-building program for young mothers. We were able to test the program's efficacy with the cooperation of the continuing education project of Medina Children's Services, Seattle. Details of our program and results of outcome evaluations follow.

Training Sessions

The skills-training program was divided into four, one-hour sessions. Three of the sessions involved teaching specific skills, and the last focused on the integrated practice of all skills. The program is adaptable to the needs of the participants and the setting in which it is presented. The training groups were led by a two-person team—one woman and one man. The female-male makeup of the team proved important during training. Our all-female participants acknowledged that interviews were more difficult for them when the prospective employers were male. Though none of our sample of young women had experienced sexual harassment, they were nonetheless ill at ease presenting themselves and their qualifications to a man. Since most of the managers we encountered during the course of the study were male, this lack of ease put our participants at a disadvantage. During the training program, all participants practiced with and received feedback from both group leaders. Discussions included direct confrontations of nervousness and discriminating between appropriate and inappropriate questions from managers. By the end of the program, participants were at ease with both men and women in job-related situations.

Though the majority of our participants were black, both group leaders were white. The present study did not directly evaluate the effects of this racial difference. On the one hand, participants might have been more relaxed and open had leaders come from their own racial and ethnic background. On the other hand, the majority of prospective employers in our community are white. In this sense, therefore, the training and practice exercises were more realistic. Sessions can be combined into a one-day workshop allowing expanded attention to certain topics. For example, appropriate/inappropriate attire and make-up could be modeled and discussed in greater detail. Helpful with individual mothers, the group approach to job-skills training presented here has several advantages. Young mothers learn from the experiences, modeling, and moral support of others. Training sessions can be condensed into one or two meetings, or presented once a week. Often, adolescent mothers have nonflexible schedules, due to the responsibilities of child care. Therefore, this kind of program may need to be delivered over a month's time or more to accommodate this group's special needs.

All four sessions in our program followed a similar format. Each session involved an introduction and review of the previous session, skill instruction and demonstrations, role-play practice, and frequent summarizations of main points. The first session presented the program's goals and demonstrated what young mothers could expect to learn. Reviews of previous sessions engaged young mothers in warm-up discussions, reinforced skills, and validated learning. Lead questions, such as, "What did you learn last time?" or "What are important points to remember from the last session?" facilitated the reviews. Throughout, the skills-training program emphasized role playing. Young mothers were divided into groups of three. Participants rotated in the role of manager, interviewee, and observer, until everyone had played each part. A handout (described under Session 2, below) assisted the person playing manager and created a realistic situation. Those playing observers offered feedback on the interviewee's performance. Feedback concentrated on emphasizing the good points in a performance and on making one suggestion for future improvement. Reinforcement from peers kept young mothers motivated and convinced them that the group members really cared about their performance.

Making training attractive to young mothers was important. Many of our participants were not committed students and disliked academic settings. We established an informal atmosphere by arranging chairs in a semicircle and by making food and drinks available. Multiple visual aids (e.g., blackboard, handouts, transparencies) increased young mothers' attention to program materials. Frequent and enthusiastic praise reinforced and increased their participation. Leaders deliberately based their demonstrations and examples on young mothers' own experiences and opinions. Even so, participants were initially reluctant to volunteer answers and to engage in role plays. Rapport and participation increased when leaders had had a chance to talk individually with each young mother. To ensure that appropriate learning was taking place, leaders frequently asked volunteers to summarize what had been covered, before moving on to the next activity. Young mothers were nervous about role playing and often complained that they "couldn't do it" or they "wouldn't say that." Leaders were supportive, but firm. They emphasized the importance of new skills for managing new life opportunities and the advantages of trying out new behavior in a practice setting before being required to use it in the real world.

The following sections describe in more detail the content of each of the training sessions.

SESSION ONE

The first session focused on introductions and on teaching teenage mothers how to use the telephone for developing job leads and setting up interviews. Because of nervousness, young mothers in our program often failed to obtain useful information over the telephone, such as the name of the manager, details about the job opening, application procedures, and leads to future openings. A second objective of Session 1 was to teach participants how to promote their skills and abilities in positive, appropriate terms.

Training exercises. Following a brief introduction about the program's objectives, young mothers were asked to give their names (for the leader's benefit) and truthfully describe themselves with one word that would appeal to an employer. On the chalk board, group leaders listed such responses as "dependable," "reliable," "motivated," and "friendly." When shy participants balked at describing themselves positively, leaders asked other group members how they might describe her (members were acquainted), thus providing her with a pool of positive information about herself. Leaders then defined skills as something a person does well because of special training or experience. Leaders asked each participant to list the specific skills she had. Young mothers were encouraged to think of skills learned by being a parent and a student, such as planning and budgeting their time and finances. If a young mother could not identify any skills, leaders helped her to explore her interests and experiences and to analyze the skills they entailed. Leaders stressed the importance of matching job skills with available openings. Teenagers are often unrealistic about selecting positions that fit their present abilities. Discussion focused on choosing an entry level position that matched current skills and could aid in further career development.

Leaders next initiated discussion of how to find out about job openings. They emphasized networking and recruiting friends and relatives to help in the job search. A form of job inquiry frequently underutilized by our participants was calling businesses about job openings. When they did make calls, teenage mothers often obtained little information beyond whether or not the business had an immediate opening. Leaders stressed the importance of asking for the manager's name and speaking directly with him or her about present and future job openings and other opportunities the manager might be able to suggest. To assist participants in developing good telephone inquiries, leaders distributed a telephone checklist (see Figure 1).* Participants were encouraged to use the checklist as a tool during their job search. Leaders provided ineffective and effective models of how to make good telephone inquiries. The ineffective model incorporated disruptive behavior such as dropping the telephone, chewing gum, sounding uninterested, getting distracted by children or pets, and failing to get crucial information (see Figure 2). Feedback was solicited from the participants on needed improvements, drawing attention to the telephone checklist and information not received.

Following the discussion, leaders modeled an appropriate telephone inquiry using the checklist. The caller's assignment was to obtain all information on the checklist. The correct model also illustrated motivation and interest in the job. After watching this demonstration, participants practiced making telephone inquiries. They divided into triads of manager, caller, and observer, and roles were rotated until each person had a chance to be the caller. The callers were told to complete the telephone checklist when they made the calls. To make the manager appear realistic, an information sheet (Figure 3) was handed out to guide the manager's responses during the call. Leaders coached participants until they had accomplished the goals of the exercise.

SESSION TWO

Session Two focused on written applications. Participants, during this session, completed a comprehensive sample application that could be referred to when filling out real applications.

Training exercises. Opening discussions focused on what constitutes work experience. Leaders listed on the board examples of paid and non-paid experiences that could be helpful toward getting a job. Leaders helped teenage mothers pinpoint life experiences that demonstrated good employee potential, such as leadership roles in church and school organizations. Some of the teenage mothers had limited paid work experience; thus, it was essential to

---

*Figures 1 through 10 appear at the end of this article.

recognize personal experiences that signified skill development. Leaders explored with the participants examples of unpaid work experience, such as volunteer work with hospitals, Girl Scout activities, or canvassing for charitable organizations.

Training focused on identifying life experiences relevant to a hiring situation and on specific descriptions of these experiences, in both written and oral communication, to a potential employer. Leaders presented basic questions that would assist an applicant in being specific. These questions included: 1) Where did you work? 2) How long did you work there? 3) When did you do this work (approximate dates)? 4) What were the duties you had to perform? Young mothers were encouraged to prepare for the job application process by rehearsing answers to these questions.

Young mothers often had relevant experience and skills, but lacked the ability to present this information accurately and concisely on a written application. Completed mock applications were presented on transparencies. Included on these applications were multiple errors (i.e., spelling, illegible handwriting, and incomplete addresses). Young mothers identified the errors and suggested improvements. Leaders clarified tricky application questions or words that caused confusion. Upon completion of the application-transparency exercise, young mothers completed application facsimilies (Figure 4). Leaders coached them to be as positive as possible. Participants handed in their applications. Leaders used a checklist (Figure 5) to review each application and make comments on its completeness. Applications and the checklist were reviewed individually with each participant and returned to them. Leaders suggested participants fill in missing information and use this application as a reference when applying for a job.

Upon completion of the exercise, leaders concluded with helpful do's and don'ts of the application process. Stress was laid on the importance of asking for an application from the manager and selecting appropriate times to pick up job applications. Lastly, participants were encouraged to complete the application at the business site, since managers agreed that this demonstrated preparation and interest in the job. Leaders reiterated the importance of providing complete, accurate information and of taking previously gathered written information to the business site.

SESSION THREE

This session provided adolescent mothers with an understanding of the interview process, the kinds of verbal and behavioral skills necessary to complete a successful interview, ways to identify and control nervousness, and ways to feel more confident in an interview.

Training exercises. Leaders began by defining the job interview as a situation in which applicants would be face-to-face with an employer, answering questions about themselves, and summarizing their skills and abilities. Interviewer expectations were discussed and group members shared their interviewing experiences. The young mothers did not recognize that hiring may be influenced by the first, largely visual impressions made by an applicant, even before the formal interview begins. Participants were informed of the importance of making a favorable impression by dressing appropriately, going alone to the interview, smiling, and behaving in a friendly but businesslike manner.

After warm-up discussion, leaders introduced the notion of body language or nonverbal behavior. Leaders' instruction focused on the kind of behavior necessary to enhance young mothers' chances for obtaining jobs. Leaders covered the content of nonverbal behavioral skills to emphasize that body actions usually communicate far more than just words, and that the consistency of verbal and nonverbal behavior is vital for an effective interview. It was noted by leaders that often young mothers' facial expressions and posture did not support what they were saying. For example, in one role play, a young mother spoke assertively about why she wanted the job, yet she did not look at the interviewer once. The lack of eye contact made the message seem insincere.

Leaders helped young mothers generate a list of effective behavioral responses important in an interview—for example, "It's good to smile and to be cordial," "Shake hands when you meet the manager," and "Sit straight in your chair." Many adolescent mothers commented that the behavior being taught did not feel natural or comfortable to them. Leaders addressed this issue by emphasizing that new, "learned" behavior which is important for job interviewing may not necessarily be useful in other situations, such as interactions with friends, relatives, or teachers. The attention paid to subjects' discomfort with the new, learned behavior is important, since people from different cultural backgrounds are taught different ways to communicate. Job getting, especially the interview portion, often requires language and behavior which seem unnatural to applicants, at least at first use. Discussion clarified these issues, increasing the young mothers' motivation to persevere with these skills.

Group instructors provided both an ineffective and an effective model of how to behave during an interview. These models incorporated both verbal and nonverbal skills. Following the ineffective model demonstration, young mothers provided feedback to the models, indicating how they could improve their performances. Then, by incorporating subjects' suggestions for improvement, leaders demonstrated an effective performance. Following the completion of the "good" model, leaders and adolescent mothers compared the two demonstrations, further reinforcing the importance of the new behavior for real life interviews.

Stress management was the next topic covered. Participants unanimously described the interview process as very anxiety provoking. This reaction accords with one author's experience with older women she has counseled, who feared looking for a job because "all I know is homemaking and parenting." Like the young mothers in the present study, most of these older women had relevant skills, but anxiety prevented them from identifying and making an effective presentation of their skills.

Leaders presented a rationale for the importance of appearing calm and confident in an interview. They pointed out, however, that some feelings of anxiety are common and in many instances may be helpful. Leaders presented a discussion on recognizing stress, the ways in which stressful feelings can affect an interview, and ways of coping with such feelings. Throughout this discussion, group members were encouraged to supply information from their previous experiences. Adolescent mothers readily recognized how stress influences an interview; for example, "If you are nervous, you fumble around for an answer, and that can make you look as though you are not prepared." Other, less visible effects of stress described by group members included perspiring a lot, and having cold and clammy hands and a dry mouth.

Stress management training focused on "self-talk." Leaders defined self-talk as comments we make to ourselves about our own behavior. Leaders provided examples of confidence destroying, self-critical self-talk, such as, "I'm so nervous about this interview. I am sure I'll mess it up." Such negative thinking adversely affects the way we present ourselves in hiring situations. On the other hand, effective self-talk, such as "Interviews aren't easy, but I made it this far. I am doing all right" affects performance positively. Leaders encouraged participants to identify and challenge their self-critical, negative thoughts and to replace them with helpful, positive ones. Figure 6 is a list of stress management tips given to participants as a handout.

The last part of the session covered typical questions asked in an interview. Leaders supplied adolescent mothers with some common interview questions. Participants' initial responses to the questions were analyzed by the whole group for their effectiveness. A frequent example of an inappropriate answer to the common interviewing question, "Why do you want this job?" was, "My parents say I have to work," or, "I guess I need a job." Examples of more effective answers were, "I'm eager to get some good experience," or, "I need the money." Figures 7 and 8 are handouts summarizing typical interview questions and helpful hints for interviewing.

SESSION FOUR

This session provided adolescent mothers with the opportunity to integrate their skills in simulated hiring situations and receive constructive feedback on their interviewing styles.

Training exercises. Leaders introduced role-play practice as a tool for preparing adolescent mothers for the actual experience of job-seeking. Practicing new behavior in a safe environment increases the chances that skills will transfer smoothly to real-life situations. Leaders again modeled typical interviews (see Figure 9) and adolescent mothers discussed the models' positive and negative aspects. The class was divided into triads of manager, interviewee, and observer. Participants playing the role of managers were required to ask questions as if they were actually hiring the person interviewing. They referred to the list in Figure 9 for ample questions. The interviewee was required to apply as many skills as possible to obtain the desired job. The triad's observer provided feedback on the interviewee's performance. The feedback consisted of reinforcing the interviewee's positive presentation of abilities and past experiences, her enthusiasm, and her communication skills, as well as suggesting ways the interviewee could improve. Leaders coached interviewees until they were successful. Leaders concluded with a brief, encouraging lecture on the "art of hanging in there." They acknowledged the difficulty of obtaining a job, the need for persistence, and the rarity of getting the first job interviewed for. Leaders encouraged adolescent mothers to learn from interviewing experiences and to think positively about their skills, abilities, and experiences, rather than to dwell on their mistakes and failures.

Evaluation and Results

Two goals directed evaluation planning. The first goal was to provide clear evidence that the job-skills training program did enhance young mothers' competitiveness in the job market. The second goal was to provide the collaborating agency and other service providers with realistic and feasible procedures for evaluating future job programs. We based the dual goals on the knowledge that valid statistical analysis of program effects often requires research procedures that are too elaborate and time-consuming for many service-oriented practitioners. The following paragraphs sketch both the formal and the informal evaluation procedures.

FORMAL EVALUATION

Before the training program began, all participants completed the following battery of assessment measures.

Multiple-Affect Adjective Checklist (M.A.A.C.L.). Following procedures suggested by Zuckerman and Lubin, the M.A.A.C.L. was given shortly before a simulated job interview to assess performance anxiety.[16] The M.A.A.C.L. is list of 132 words that refer to personal feelings—examples include "annoyed," "calm," "fine," "joyful," "nervous," "secure," and "shaky." So as not to overtax our participants, we reduced the word list to sixty-one. We instructed them to check all the words that described how they felt at the present moment.

Employment Application Form. Each young mother completed an employment application consisting of closed-ended questions on her personal background, academic record, and previous employment history, and open-ended questions on criminal convictions, outstanding debts, and health (see Figure 4). Employment applications were scored by two personnel specialists responsible for hiring and job placement in two community businesses. Specialists awarded all applications numerical scores quantifying attributes of neatness, competence, academic qualifications, employment history, and recommendation for hiring/placement.

Audiotaped Telephone Call. Leaders gave each participant a card with a telephone number to call to get more information about a job opportunity. Participants were audiotaped as they dialed and conducted a role-played call to the prospective employer. Telephones borrowed from the local telephone company were hooked to each other to approximate a real call without going through public phone lines. A researcher on the second phone supplied standardized responses to all questions and comments from the callers. Raters scored the phone conversations for young mothers' ability to get relevant information about the job and the application process, and to set up an interview appointment for themselves.

Videotaped Job Interview. After completing the employment application and the phone call, the young women were individually videotaped in a role-played job interview. The prospective "employer" was male. Over a ten-minute period, an interviewer asked each participant about her educational and employment background, career goals, and general personality characteristics. Interviews were scored by four raters quantifying nonverbal skills of eye contact and smiles, and verbal skills of positive self-statements, negative self-statements, unspecific responses, and nonresponses. Raters took absolute frequency counts for all skills except eye contact, which was scored as total seconds of eye contact with interviewer.

After completing the pretraining assessment measures, participants were randomly assigned to either a discussion group focusing on vocational choice and jobs in general or to the job-skills training program described above. The number and length of sessions were identical for both groups. At the end of training, all participants completed the assessment battery again.

RESULTS

Comparing pretest to posttest changes between the two

groups quantified effects attributable to training. Analyses showed consistently more positive changes for the training-program participants than for discussion group participants. Young mothers who received job-skills training were less anxious as measured by the Multiple Affect Adjective Checklist. Personnel specialists rated their written employment applications as more complete and containing more relevant academic qualifications and better employment histories than those of discussion group participants. In the telephone and personal interview situations, young mothers given job-skills training had more desirable changes in eye contact, smiles, direct information-getting statements, and positive self-statements as compared with discussion group members. Trained young women also significantly decreased their negative, unspecific, and inapropriate comments.

Follow-up to assess the relevance of these skills for actually getting a job was complicated by the fact that 25% of the participants were pregnant at the time of the study and, for a number of months, would be at a special—though temporary—disadvantage in the job market. Also, at the collaborating agency's request, we agreed to give job-skills training ultimately to all the discussion group participants, thus making any long-term comparisons between the two groups meaningless. To gain a consistent and controlled evaluation of all participants' chances for employment, we requested the help of managers and personnel specialists in large and small businesses in the community who routinely made hiring decisions at the entry level. Substituting code numbers for names on young mothers' posttraining assessment materials, we gave assessment materials completed by all our subjects at posttest to our community specialists. Since the discussion group participants had not yet received the training program, comparison of the two groups could demonstrate the effectiveness of our training program for enhancing subjects' chances for getting a job. We asked the managers to state whether they would or would not recommend each applicant for an entry level job in their organization. Significantly, the group of young mothers who completed the job-skills training received "recommend for hiring" ratings nearly ten times more often than did discussion group participants.

Although we believe that evaluation of treatment effectiveness is an important component of all service giving, we know that control and comparison groups and elaborate assessment procedures are beyond the resources of many practitioners who work with pregnant and parenting adolescents. The next section outlines less formal approaches to evaluation that we have used successfully in continuing the agency-based job-skills training program for young women.

LESS FORMAL EVALUATION

Because many service practitioners work with individuals as opposed to groups, single-subject evaluation procedures can be most helpful. Single-subject designs allow for the evaluation of one client's changes over time.[17] This method can be used with a single measure or with multiple measures, such as questionnaire(s), audiotapes, videotapes, and live interviews. The use of multiple measures can increase the precision of the skills assessment. But one or two measures may be more realistic and feasible for the service-providing practitioner. The following example clarifies how single-subject evaluations are used.

Cindy Montoya is a 17-year-old Hispana. Two direct measures were used to evaluate Ms. Montoya's job-getting skills. These were the audiotaped telephone call and the videotaped job interview discussed above. A third, less direct measure—a self-esteem questionnaire—was selected to assess Montoya's confidence level and her personal self-image. The rationale for this measure is the thesis that self-esteem directly affects attitudes and the ability to handle a job search effectively. If a young mother is negative about herself and her experiences, she will downplay her abilities during an interview, thus decreasing her chances for getting a job. Sample self-esteem items used were, "On the whole I am satisfied with myself" and "I wish I could have more respect for myself." Each question was to be answered with either a Strongly Agree, Agree, Disagree, or Strongly Disagree.

Testing Cindy Montoya's skill and attitude levels before and after the job-skills training helped her instructors see the progress she made, as well as which parts of the program were effective. In all three of the areas measured, Montoya showed improvement from pre- to post-assessment. Figure 10 summarizes her scores. Rather than employing statistical calculations, scores were simply graphed and visually inspected for relevant changes. Montoya herself rated the job program's utility and success from her perspective. On a 6-point scale (6 equaling a high rating and 1 a low rating), she scored the job-skills program in terms of how useful it was, how enjoyable it was, and how likely she would be to recommend this program to a friend. Participants consistently awarded the program high scores. If audio- or videotaping proves too cumbersome, written job application measures can be substituted. Long-term follow-up to assess whether trainees get and keep jobs can be difficult for service providers, often because young women terminate their association with the agency shortly after training. If this is the case, it would be worthwhile to use assessment materials to solicit hirability ratings from employers in the community to document the program's effectiveness.

FIGURE 1

Telephone Checklist

	1	2	3
HAVE READY			
1. Paper and pencil.			
2. List of places to call and telephone numbers.			
DO			
1. Speak clearly.			
2. Speak politely.			
3. Give your name.			
ASK			
1. For the manager's name (WRITE IT DOWN).			
2. To speak to the manager.			
3. If they are hiring.			
4. What positions are available.			
5. If no openings now, when will they be hiring.			
6. What are the applications procedures (Will you need to fill out an application? Will you need an interview appointment?)			
7. Where to apply.			
8. The best time to apply.			
9. To set up an interview appointment.			

FIGURE 2

Incorrect Model Telephone Vignette
(Leaders: Chew gum, become distracted.)

Employee: "McDonald's. May I help you?"

Caller: "Uh, yeah, say, you got any jobs open?"

Employee: "I'm not the one you should speak to. I'll get the manager."

Manager: "This is the manager speaking. What can I help you with?"

Caller:	"Uh, well, got any job openings down there? Oh, wait, hold on (put hand over receiver, mumble, return): "Yeah, O.K. What was it? Oh, hiring anyone?"
Manager:	"If you come in and fill out an application, we'll discuss the possibility."
Caller:	"Umm, I'm not so sure I wanna come all the way on down there if you can't tell me if I can get a job."
Manager:	"You must fill out an application first. Come between 2:00 and 4:00 P.M. tomorrow. Don't come any other time, I'll be busy.
Caller:	"Well, umm . . ., O.K., maybe I'll be by if I can get a sitter.
Manager:	"Good afternoon!" (Hang up!)

FIGURE 3

Manager Information Sheet

Company name: Vip's.

My name is Jane Rawlings.

We have openings for a short-order cook, two waitress positions, a dishwasher, and busboy.

We are taking applications at the downtown location. That's at 4th and Blanchard.

We will take applications only between 9:00 and 11 A.M. next Thursday.

I'm not making appointments for interviews until I've taken in all the applications and looked them over. We'll call you back if we want you to interview.

FIGURE 4

Application

Name _____
        Last   First   Middle   Social Security #

Present address: _____
                  Number   Street   City   State   Zip

Permanent address: _____
                    Number   Street   City   State   Zip

Home phone: _____ Birthdate: _____

Do you have any illness, injury, physical, or mental conditions which might inter-
    fere with performing certain kinds of work?   Yes _____   No _____

If yes, describe in full:_____

Have you been convicted of a crime in the last 7 years (excluding non-moving traf-
    fic violations)?   Yes _____   No _____

If yes, please specify charges, locations, dates, and penalties:

_____

Person to contact in case of emergency:

_____
        Name   Address   Telephone

Can you provide proof of citizenship, visa, or alien registration?
    _____ Yes _____ No

Are you a veteran?   _____ Yes _____ No

EMPLOYMENT DESIRED

Position applying for: _____

Date you can start: _____ _____ Part-time _____ Full-time

Are you able to work nights? _____ Yes _____ No   Weekends: _____ Yes _____ No

What led you to contact us?_____

Ever applied to, or worked for, this company before?   _____ Yes _____ No

    If yes, where: _____ From: _____ To: _____

    Supervisor's name: _____ Reason for leaving: _____

Do you have transportation to get to work?   _____ Yes _____ No

If hired, do you agree to abide by safety rules of the company? _____ Yes _____ No

PERSONAL REFERENCES (other than family and employers):

Name	Address	Telephone
Name	Address	Telephone
Name	Address	Telephone

EDUCATION

School Name & Address	From/To Mo/Yr	Diploma	Major	GPA
High:				
Trade:				
College:				

Phone number of last school attended: _____

Name of teacher/counselor: _____

Extracurricular activities in school: _____

Have you had any training other than as indicated under "school" above? _____ Yes _____ No

If yes, please describe: _____

WORK HISTORY
(List below last four employers, starting with most recent, first.)

1. Employer: _____   Phone: _____
   Address: _____   From: _____ To: _____
   City/State: _____ Zip: ____ Salary: _____
   Duties: _____   Full-Time: _____ Part-Time: _____
   Reason for leaving: _____ Hours per week: _____

2. Employer: _____   Phone: _____
   Address: _____   From: _____ To: _____
   City/State: _____ Zip: ____ Salary: _____
   Duties: _____   Full-Time: _____ Part-Time: _____
   Reason for leaving: _____ Hours per week: _____

3. Employer: _____ Phone: _____

Address: _____ From: _____ To: _____

City/State: _____ Zip: _____ Salary: _____

Duties: _____ Full-Time: ____ Part-Time: ____

Reason for leaving: _____ Hours per week: _____

4. Employer: _____ Phone: _____

Address: _____ From: _____ To: _____

City/State: _____ Zip: _____ Salary: _____

Duties: _____ Full-Time: ____ Part-Time: ____

Reason for leaving: _____ Hours per week: _____

Describe your skills and abilities:

I certify that the information provided by me in this application is true and correct to the best of my knowledge. I hereby authorize a confidential investigation of my background including my work performance with previous employers, to determine my qualifications for employment.

_____ _____
Date Signature

FIGURE 5

Job Application Checklist

PERSONAL FACTS   COMMENTS

- ☐ Listed name in correct order.   _____
- ☐ Complete addresses.   _____
- ☐   include street address (Ave., Pl.).   _____
- ☐   apartment # (if approp.).   _____
- ☐   zip codes.   _____
- ☐ Identified person to contact in emergency.   _____
- ☐   address.   _____
- ☐   telephone number.   _____
- ☐ Indicated birth date.   _____
- ☐ Answered question regarding: health.   _____

EDUCATION

- ☐ Listed schools attended in order requested.   _____
- ☐   list full name of school.   _____
- ☐   indicated addresses and telephone.   _____
- ☐   identified years attended.   _____
- ☐ Indicated school activities and interests.   _____

WORK EXPERIENCE

- ☐ Listed past employers beginning with present.   _____
- ☐   address included (Street, Ave., Pl.).   _____
- ☐   include zip code.   _____
- ☐   include telephone # (area code, if necessary).   _____
- ☐ Described position held.   _____
- ☐ Indicated dates of employment.   _____
- ☐ Indicated reason for leaving.   _____
- ☐ Entered wage earned.   _____
- ☐ Indicated hours worked.   _____
- ☐ Indicated full or part-time employment.   _____

REFERENCES

☐ Listed 3 people who are *not* past employers or family.   _____
☐   address included (St., Ave., Pl.).   _____
☐   included zip code.   _____
☐   included telephone # (area code, if necessary).   _____

MISCELLANEOUS

☐ Answered all other questions.   _____
☐ Spelling correct.   _____
☐ Printed clearly.   _____
☐ Signed and dated application.   _____
☐ Described skills and abilities.   _____

NOTES

FIGURE 6

Stress Management Tips

INTERVIEW PREPARATION

1. Pick out wardrobe night before interview.
2. Start early working on personal grooming.
3. Make all necessary child care arrangements in advance.
4. Review the interview question list.
5. Practice interview questions and making positive comments about yourself either with a friend, relative, or even in front of a mirror.
6. Get directions to place of interview ahead of time, and know them well.
7. Get a good night's sleep.

RELAXATION
(could be done at home, in waiting room, or even in a bus or a car)

1. Arrive at interview early.
2. Sit in comfortable chair or couch:
   • Place hands in your lap.
   • Close your eyes or stare at your knees.
3. Take three long deep breaths. Slowly inhale through your nose and slowly exhale through your mouth.

4. Now tell yourself some positive things:
    - "I can handle this."
    - "I am prepared."
    - "I'll do the best I can."
    - "Whatever happens is O.K."
5. Remember some feelings of nervousness are O.K., and can even help your performance.

FIGURE 7

Interview Questions

QUESTIONS YOU MIGHT BE ASKED IN AN INTERVIEW:

1. Why are you qualified for this job?
2. Have you ever done this kind of work before?
3. Why do you want to work here?
4. How is your health?
5. Why should we hire you instead of someone else?
6. When are you available for work?
7. What kinds of machines or equipment can you operate?
8. Why did you apply for this job?
9. What kind of salary do you need?
10. What are your goals?
11. How would you describe yourself?
12. What are your strengths?
13. What are your weaknesses?
14. Tell me about yourself.
15. What relevant experience have you had?
16. What was your favorite class in school? Why?
17. How do you handle pressure on the job or in school?
18. What do you think it takes to be successful?
19. What two or three accomplishments in your life have given you the most satisfaction?
20. What is your previous work experience?
21. What did you like best about your last job?
22. What did you like least about your last job?
23. Do you have any questions?

FIGURE 8

Helpful Hints for Job Interviewing

Do's

1. Do get a good night's sleep before the interview. You will be more alert and make a better impression.
2. Do find out ahead of time exactly where you will have the interview, how to get there, and how long it will take you.
3. Do get to the interview early. This shows that you are reliable.
4. Do phone the interviewer if you cannot go to the interview and ask to reschedule the interview. Do this only if you have a real problem, like being sick.
5. Do know how to pronounce the interviewer's name. This makes the interviewer feel good. If the name is hard to pronounce, ask the interviewer how to say it.
6. Do shake hands with the interviewer when the interview starts and when it ends.
7. Do look at the interviewer when you talk. This shows that you are sure of yourself.
8. Do sit up straight during the interview. You will look more interested in the interview and the job.
9. Do dress nicely for the interview. A neat, clean appearance says you care about yourself and the job.
10. Do take your practice application with you to the interview. Then you will have no difficulty in completing a job application. Be sure it is complete and current.
11. Do find out some things about an employer before you go to an interview. For example: Does the employer manufacture? Does the employer provide services? What are the services? Your interest shows that you care about the company and the job.
12. Do review the interview questions handout and prepare answers to questions which you can anticipate in the interview.
13. Do interview alone. This shows more self-reliance.

Don'ts

1. Don't sit down in the interviewer's office until the interviewer asks you to.
2. Don't look at your watch during the interview. The interviewer may think you do not want to spend much time at the interview.
3. Don't talk while the interviewer is reading your application. The interviewer may have trouble reading if you talk.
4. Don't call the interviewer by his/her first name. Use the person's last name.

5. Don't chew gum or smoke at the interview. This distracts from a calm, confident appearance. Even if the interviewer says that you may smoke, you *still* should not smoke.

6. Don't wear your sunglasses, hat, or outdoor coat during the interview. Take them off when you arrive for the interview.

7. Don't wear too much makeup, jewelry, or perfume to the interview. These can be distracting and can hurt your chances of getting the job.

8. Don't ask right away about pay, working hours, or benefits. Wait until the interviewer brings up these things. Then you can ask questions. It is better to discuss your qualifications and experience first.

FIGURE 9

Model Interview

(Interviewee standing, knocks on back of chair. Manager starts.)

Manager: Come in.

Interviewee: Hi, Mr. Sherman. I am _____. I am here to see you about the hostess job.

Manager: (Stands up, extends hand for hand shaking.) Hello, _____. Please sit down.

Interviewee: (Sits down.) Thank you.

Manager: O.K. I will begin by telling you about the job. We need someone for dinner hours only. The hostess is expected to take reservations, greet and seat the guests, and answer the phone. Also, we have a dress code, that requires you to wear a uniform. (Pause.) Do you have any questions?

Interviewee: Yes, I do. What specifically are the dinner hours you mentioned, and for what days of the week are you hiring a hostess?

Manager: The hours are 5:00–9:00 P.M., Monday, Wednesday, Friday, and Saturday.

Interviewee: O.K. (Nods head.)

Manager: I would like to know more about you. What experiences have you had that qualify you for this position?

Interviewee: Well. For the past year, I have been responsible for the seating arrangements at my church's monthly suppers. Usually about forty to fifty people attend. I am a student at Garfield High and for the past two semesters I have worked in the school office. Part of my duties have been to answer the phone and take messages for the principal.

Manager: What are the things you liked best about your job at the school?

Interviewee:	The principal depends on me, and I like handling the responsibility. Also, I like greeting the people that come into the office.
Manager:	I see, tell me, why do you want to work here?
Interviewee:	I like this type of work, and I feel I can do a good job. The hours fit in well with my school schedule. Also, you are close to my home, so transportation is not a problem.
Manager:	We serve a lot of families here, and the dinner hour gets pretty busy with so many children. Have you had much experience with kids?
Interviewee:	As a matter of fact, I have two children of my own. I've learned to have a lot of patience with them, and I've become very creative at handling them during meal time.
Manager:	I'm curious. Give me an example of a creative way of handling your children.
Interviewee:	Well, a couple of things that work with my kids is giving them a cracker while they wait for dinner to be served and then letting them color while they wait for the grown-ups to finish.
Manager:	Great! (Pause.) Don't you think that caring for your children will interfere with the work schedule here?
Interviewee:	I have thought about that and I have made arrangements for child care. This job is important to me, and I am a very conscientious person.
Manager:	Thank you. I will let you know my decision by the end of the week. (Manager stands up, extends hand for hand shake.)
Interviewee:	(Stands up, shakes hands with manager.) Thank you, Mr. Sherman. I will be looking forward to hearing from you.

FIGURE 10

Single-Subject Scores

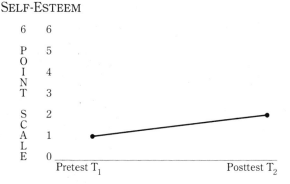

SELF-ESTEEM

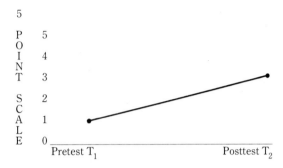

OVERALL RATING ON TELEPHONE SKILLS

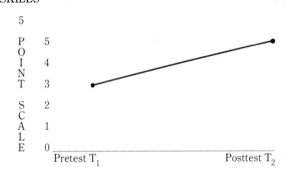

OVERALL RATING ON PERSONAL INTERVIEWING SKILLS

NOTES

1. United States Department of Labor, Bureau of Labor Statistics, *School and Work Among Youth During the 1970's* (Special Labor Force Report 241). Washington, D.C.: U.S. Department of Labor, 1981.

2. United States Department of Labor, Bureau of Labor Statistics, *Employment in Perspective: Minority Workers* (Report 652). Washington, D.C.: U.S. Department of Labor, 1981.

3. Coalition on Women and the Budget, *Inequality of Sacrifice: The Impact of the Reagan Budget on Women* (Washington, D.C., March 16, 1983), p. 26.

4. United States Department of Labor, Bureau of Labor Statistics, *School and Work Among Youth During the 1970's*. (Special Labor Force Report 241). Washington, D.C.: U.S. Department of Labor, 1981.

5. Harriet B. Presser, *Social Consequences of Teenage Childbearing*, paper presented at the Conference on the Consequences of Adolescent Pregnancy and Childbearing, Bethesda, Maryland, October 1975.

6. Lloyd Bacon, "Early Motherhood, Accelerated Role Transition, and Social Pathologies," *Social Forces* 52 (1974), pp. 333–341.

7. Joyce O. Beckett, "Working Wives: A Racial Comparison," *Social Work* 21 (November 1976), pp. 463–471; Marcia Friedman, "Jobs Called No. 1 Issue for Blacks," *Seattle Post–Intelligencer* (May 12, 1982), p. A5.

8. Kristin A. Moore, "Teenage Childbirth and Welfare Dependency," *Family Planning Perspectives* 10 (July/August 1978), pp. 233–235.

9. Denise F. Polit, Janet R. Kahn, Charles A. Murray, and Kevin W. Smith, *Needs and Characteristics of Pregnant and Parenting Teens, The Baseline Report for Project Redirection* (New York: Manpower Demonstration Research Corporation, 1982).

10. Melvin Zelnik and John F. Kantner, "First Pregnancies to Women Aged 15–19: 1976 and 1971," *Family Planning Perspectives* 10 (January/February, 1978), pp. 11–20; and Douglass F. Clapp and Rebecca Staude Raab, "Follow-Up of Unmarried Adolescent Mothers," *Social Work* 23 (March 1978), pp. 149–153.

11. Denise F. Polit *et al.*

12. Joel R. Barbee and Ellsworth C. Keil, "Experimental Techniques of Job Interview Training for the Disadvantaged: Videotape Feedback, Behavior Modification, and Microcounseling," *Journal of Applied Psychology* 58 (October 1973), pp. 209–213; Richard G. Heimberg, Jerry Cunningham, Judy Stanley, and Richard Blankenberg, "Preparing Unemployed Youth for Job Interviews," *Behavior Modification* 6 (July 1982), pp. 299–322; Ellsworth C. Keil and Joel R. Barbee, "Behavior Modification and Training the Disadvantaged Job Interviewee," *Vocational Guidance Quarterly* 22 (September 1973), pp. 50–56; C. Dean Miller and Gene Oetting, "Barriers to Employment and the Disadvantaged," *Personnel and Guidance Journal* 56 (October 1977), pp. 89–93; Denise F. Polit *et al.*

13.   H.A. Becker, "The Assertive Job-Hunting Survey," *Measurement and Evaluation in Guidance* 13 (January 1980), pp. 43–48.

14.   Barbee and Keil, "Experimental Techniques," p. 209.

15.   A.G. Billings and R.H. Moos, "The Role of Coping Responses and Social Resources in Attentuating the Stress of Life Events," *Journal of Behavioral Medicine* 4 (Winter, 1981), pp. 139–157; L.I. Pearlin and C. Schooler, "The Structure of Coping," *Journal of Health and Social Behavior* 19 (1978), pp. 2–21.

16.   Marvin Zuckerman and B. Lubin, *Manual for the Multiple Affect Adjective Checklist* (San Diego: Educational and Industrial Testing Service, 1965).

17.   Sirika Jayaratne and Rona L. Levy, *Empirical Clinical Practice* (New York: Columbia University Press, 1979).

"Si Necesita Ayuda, Llame. . . .": Counseling for Latina Rape Survivors

Teresa Contreras and Irene D. Mendez

Background: the East Los Angeles Rape Hotline

Like other rape crisis centers of the period, the East Los Angeles Rape Hotline originated, in 1975, in a voluntary effort. As director of the Eastside Multi-Service Center in Los Angeles, Irene Mendez was receiving a large number of referrals of Spanish-speaking clients from other agencies. Many referrals came from Connie Destito, a social worker providing support services to sexual assault victims entering the emergency room of the Los Angeles County Women's Hospital. Together, these two women set out to establish a bilingual rape hotline. They developed a curriculum for training counselors, and, from friends, colleagues, and community contacts, recruited over a dozen women for the bilingual training program. The same group of women banded together to raise funds for the expenses of the twenty-four-hour emergency line, also securing a one-room office and C.E.T.A.* staff.

Initially, volunteers and staff wore several hats, serving as counselors, advocates, and board members. They provided the

---

C.E.T.A.: Comprehensive Employment and Training Act.

woman-power for serving the victims – or, in the more positive terms of the Hotline, the "survivors" – and for directing the activities and growth of the organization.[1] Linkages were established with community organizations, public and private mental health agencies, public and private medical facilities, and law enforcement agencies, for the exchange of referrals.

A second group of volunteers was trained, expanding further the network of individuals committed to the Hotline and to its mission of offering not merely Spanish/English services, but a thoroughly bicultural approach. Meanwhile, husbands, boyfriends, and other male friends and relatives expressed interest in supporting the new organization. After analyzing and discussing the needs of the Hotline and the community it served, its Chicana feminist leaders arrived at a deliberate decision to include men in its programs of education and support. Their emerging philosophy identified concern about sexual assault as based on humanistic principles held by both women and men. In articulating this viewpoint in their community, they felt that they could call upon the importance attached by Latinos[2] to *la familia,* emphasizing for men the positive concept of *hombre,* rather than the negative *macho.*[3] Beyond these considerations, the position chosen by the Hotline accords with that of other organized Third World/women of color who have wished to demonstrate solidarity, in an oppressive society, with the male members of their group.

Out of the conglomerate of persons attracted to the Hotline came additional fundraisers, publicity agents, and grant writers. The first result of strengthened activities was a $1000 grant from a local Presbyterian Church. Approximately a year later, a $5000 grant was secured from the California State Department of Social Services. That grant was later increased to $10,000 and administered out of the California State Office of Criminal Justice and Planning (O.C.J.P.). Since 1981, the Hotline has continued to be partially funded by the O.C.J.P. The O.C.J.P. also awarded the Hotline a separate grant to develop a *fotonovela,* a photo magazine focusing on misconceptions about sexual assault, family responses to the crime of rape, and information about the resources available to the survivor, her family, and friends.

The Hotline remains a basically grassroots organization, dependent upon the support it generates in the community, and, with few paid staff, powered mainly by volunteers. Some volunteer counselor/advocates have worked with the Hotline since its inception; other early workers now serve as consultants, board members, and donors, alongside newer recruits. A vital community resource, the Hotline continues to be the only bilingual, bicultural service of its kind in the State of California. Although its primary service area is Greater East Los Angeles, its bilingual capacity generates calls from all areas of Los Angeles County.

A Diverse Population

Addressing the issue of rape in a predominantly Latino community poses special challenges. Latinos are not a homogenous group. The term *Latino* includes people of Mexican, Puerto Rican, and Cuban descent, as well as people from other Central and Latin American countries. In Los Angeles, the diversity of the Latino population is evident in varying income and educational levels, lifestyles, manner of coping with stress, family patterns, residency status, length of time in this country, and languages spoken. Latinos range from those who adhere strictly to traditional cultural practices to those who have totally assimilated Anglo-American values and customs. In the middle are those who have blended the values and customs of both cultures.

Despite the tremendous diversity among Latina women, some general characteristics were noted by Hotline staff to exist among the victims/clients. One can divide them into two broad categories, which we have designated for convenience as *Latina* and *Chicana*.

LATINA

- Primarily or exclusively Spanish-speaking
- Reared in Mexico, Latin America, Puerto Rico, or Cuba
- Little or no North American acculturation
- Agency-referred to Hotline
- Unfamiliar with medical and legal procedures
- Major concern with loss of chastity or virginity (particularly relevant to adolescents)
- Primary emotional reactions of shame, guilt, and loss
- Involved extensively with sexual aspect of the crime
- Lack of accurate sex information
- Concern regarding residency status

- Tends not to report the crime
- Vague articulation of assault and her feelings
- Uses body language as a significant way of conveying feelings

CHICANA

- Primarily English-speaking
- Reared in the United States
- Some or much acculturation
- Tends to be self-referred to Hotline
- More familiar with medical and legal procedures
- Direct and focused articulation of assault and feelings
- Verbal manner of conveying information

Special Cultural Considerations

How does the Latina react to the rape trauma? What are the special difficulties she experiences as a rape survivor? While definitive research in this area is lacking, the traditional cultural patterns provide some preliminary answers.

Rape has always been a threat to women. Historically, Latino men seem to have responded to this threat by keeping women confined to the safety of their homes. In extreme cases, women were not allowed to leave their homes without an escort, whether that be a child, brother or some other relative. Thus, the Latina woman was taught to see the world as a hostile place to be avoided. Vestiges of this world view are most apparent in immigrant women from Latin America and are still visible, in spite of acculturation, in many Chicanas' self perceptions and role expectations. A Latina who ventures into a prohibited environment may therefore hold herself responsible for any harm that befalls her. The victim of gang rape in East Los Angeles often sees her assault as a consequence of having crossed into a non-home territory dominated by an unfamiliar gang.

The traditional view of female/male roles in the Latino culture also has a significant influence on the Latina's reaction to rape. In the Latino culture, as in other cultures, men are expected to be powerful in relation to women and to prove their sexual prowess. The Latina, on the other hand, is conditioned to accept the values of chastity, self-sacrifice, yielding to others, family interdependence, and dedication to the home. The sexually active Latina is

viewed as wanton and therefore responsible if sexual assault occurs. If the woman is a virgin, less responsibility may be attributed
directly to her. However, her reputation and marriageability are
viewed as compromised; therefore, she may be subject to severe
self-criticism as well as the criticism and anger of her family.

In the Latino cultural and religious perspective, human sexuality is confined to marriage and procreation, and is considered a
very private matter. This view is the foundation of numerous sexual taboos and of the sexual interpretation of rape. The Latino emphasis on virginity for a single woman and on chastity for a married
one plays an important part in the Latina's feelings of self-respect
and her expectations of respect from others. She will generally in-
terpret a sexual assault as a sexual incident bringing shame, dis-
honor, and loss of respect for her and her family.

The Latino view of rape as a sexual act, particularly the interpretation of rape as God's punishment for some previous sin, arises
from the influence of the Catholic Church on Latino culture. The
Church ideal of woman's virginity and purity of mind and body
plays a dominant role in cultural attitudes toward sexuality and
rape. The Latina who is raped, consequently, often not only believes that she has committed a sin by having sex with a partner to
whom she is not married, but that she is either being punished by
God for something terrible that she has done in the past, or that she
will be punished because she was raped. Her sense of guilt is ag-
gravated if she did not "resist" the rape.

A Primarily Youthful Clientele

Hotline crisis intervention serves an average of thirty to forty
sexual assault survivors a month. The age of survivors ranges from
five years old to seventy. However, the majority of callers are
young women aged sixteen to twenty-three, and/or the families of
youthful victims.[4] Cultivating appropriate services for this population has therefore been a Hotline priority.

The young survivor is peculiarly vulnerable to the common experiences of rejection, chastisement, alienation, and isolation. Accustomed to the domination of the family, moreover, traditionally
reared Latina young women view authority as lying outside themselves. They have been taught that personal choices and desires
must be forfeited to respect for parents and elders. The concept of

individual or female "rights" in decision-making therefore may have little force with the very youthful Latina. These factors — which also operate strongly among the more adult, less acculturated Latina clients — frequently stand in the way of the victim's making choices which may be seen as "best" or "better" by counselor/advocates.

A variety of additional factors special to the Latina rape survivor have also come to the attention of Hotline practitioners.

Circumstances of Assaults

In recent years, much headway has been made by the anti-rape movement in combatting the misconception of rape as a sexual act and identifying sexual assault as a crime of violence. The violence of rape is quite evident in the experiences of the Latina survivors cared for through the Hotline. However, the circumstances in which Latinas are likely to become victims of rape are somewhat different from those of the population at large. In the general population, 45 percent of women reporting rape are assaulted in their homes. Sixty-seven percent of rape survivors know the identity of the person raping them, and it is commonly an acquaintance. The rapist is generally of the same race or ethnic group as his victim.

Many of the Latinas who have received aid from the Hotline and the Los Angeles County Women's Hospital have not been raped in their homes, with the exception of child sexual assault and molestation victims. Some of the survivors claimed to have been raped by gangs, by "coyotes" (transporters of undocumented workers), by immigration officials, and, particularly in the case of factory and domestic workers, by their bosses or work supervisors.

Although little is known about the gang rape phenomenon in the East Los Angeles community, information contacts with gang-affiliated female adolescents have revealed that gang rapes occur more frequently than is manifested by police or sheriff reports. John M. MacDonald, in *Rape Offenders and Their Victims,* finds that the Latina is ten times more likely to be a gang rape victim than the white woman.[5] Shame, humiliation, or fear of reprisal by gang members contribute to the low rate of reported gang rapes.

Case Histories

A few case histories collected by the Hotline illustrate the violent and devastating effect of rape on the Latina.

CASE 1.

Anna, a fourteen-year-old Mexican girl, was brought to the emergency room of the hospital, after having been raped by four teenage gang members. It was learned that a police report has been taken after a call from school authorities. The police sent Anna to the hospital for a medical examination and collection of evidence.

Anna's mother was reluctant to be at the hospital, and her anger toward her daughter was evident. The mother indicated that her daughter had shamed and humiliated the family. Additionally, she now felt threatened by the involvement of the legal authorities because of the family's undocumented residency status. Furthermore, the family was being harassed by the gang. The mother blamed her daughter, rationalizing that had she not been absent from school, the whole incident would never have occurred.

Within a few days, a preliminary hearing was held. The mother refused to go; instead, a social worker accompanied Anna to court. Young friends of the victim, witnesses to the alleged assault, had been subpoenaed. They were very supportive, under the circumstances. The witnesses were frightened, because some of them were illegal immigrants and they, too, were being threatened by the gang. Their parents were angry with Anna and no longer wanted their children to associate with her. Some parents felt sure she had seduced the boys. All of the parents were angry at having to participate in these shameful legal proceedings.

After two days of hearings, the gang members were found guilty. However, it had seemed as if it was Anna who was on trial. She sat through two days of questioning by four defending attorneys. She had to answer specific, technical questions about the sexual act, until then a little known and taboo subject for Anna. Not only had her body been violently assaulted, but her sense of dignity had also been violated. In addition to her negative feelings about herself, she had to contend with the anger and fear of her family and friends. In the end, even with the conviction of the rapists, Anna felt literally ruined.

CASE 2.

A recent arrival from Guatemala went to the local Planned Parenthood office to get an abortion. She seemed unusually upset about the abortion and was crying. After some probing by the social worker, she indicated that she was seeking the abortion as a result of being raped on her journey to the United States from Guatemala. When asked why she did not report the incident to the immigration officials, she indicated that it had been an immigration official who had raped her. The entire incident left this woman feeling defiled and ashamed. For this reason, she did not want to continue the resulting pregnancy, yet she felt very guilty about the abortion.

Through tears the woman explained that she had come to the United States to seek a better life and to improve herself, only to have this awful thing happen to her. She felt that she had done wrong in leaving her family in Guatemala, and viewed the rape as God's way of punishing her for deserting them. Now that she was having the abortion, she felt that she was a "bad" woman and that God was going to punish her for killing her child.

CASE 3.

The Hotline received a telephone call from a young Spanish-speaking woman who did not want to identify herself. She was sobbing, and at first it was difficult to understand her. The counselor soothed the young woman, telling her to cry it out before she tried to talk. At last, the young woman was able to tell the counselor that although someone had given her the Hotline number, she felt that there was nothing that anyone could do to help her. After a few questions, her story began to unfold.

This young woman had been working in a factory somewhere on the West side of Los Angeles. There were many women like her working there. They were without immigration papers and, in order to keep their jobs, felt forced to do anything the supervisor asked of them. He was a middle-aged Chicano who, whenever he wished, would ask one of the women to stay after work. He would then rape her. The women in the factory all knew what was going on, and each one lived in fear of being the next victim. However, no one dared report the supervisor, out of fear of losing their jobs and being deported. The night of this young woman's call, it had been her turn. Like the other women, she felt trapped and desperate to find someone to whom she could turn for help.

CASE 4.

Clara was a factory worker who called the Hotline after she was raped. The man who had raped her was a co-worker who had started wooing her some time earlier. She was interested in him, but was ashamed to tell him that she had a child born out of wedlock, in Mexico. In fact, she had come to the United States from Mexico with her brother because her chances of marrying in Mexico had been shattered. When the young man asked Clara for a date, she told him—as was consistent with her traditional upbringing—that she wanted him first to meet her brother and ask his permission to take her out.

One evening, the woman with whom Clara carpooled became ill and left work early, leaving Clara without a ride home. The young man offered to take her home, pointing out that this would be a good opportunity for him to meet her brother. On the way home, however, he drove her to a deserted spot and raped her. Her screams attracted someone's attention, and the police were called to the scene and arrested the rapist. It is doubtful that Clara would have reported the rape had the crime not come to the attention of the police.

As the trial date approached, Clara began to have doubts about pressing charges. The young man had begun to telephone her. He expressed his feelings of regret about the incident, telling her that he loved her and wanted to marry her. He had found out about her child, and promised to adopt him so that they could become a real family. Since Clara already felt tainted because of the out-of-wedlock status of the child, it was easy for her to believe that the rape had occurred because she was a "used" woman. She felt that marriage offered her a chance to become an "honest woman," able to hold up her head in the community. Clara dropped the charges and began preparations for her impending marriage. However, the young man never called her again.

Reaching the Latina Survivor

The Latina victim of sexual assault may experience consider-able conflict about seeking help. Few agencies provide bilingual/bicultural services. Further, agency services may not seem rele-vant to the Latina, for her socialization has conditioned her to de-pend on her extended family in times of crisis. An adolescent Latina may be in special conflict because of the authority of par-ents and her greater economic and emotional dependence on the family. Yet because of the strong taboos that surround sexuality in the Latino culture, the rape victim may feel unable to turn to her family for help.

For many Latinas, it is not only shame or humiliation that pre-vents their seeking assistance, but also a fear of deportation. The feared deportation may come in the form of immediate arrest be-cause of the Latina's undocumented status, or in the form of repri-sal by the assailant if, for example, he is her employer or co-worker.

Thus, for the Latina, disclosure of the sexual assault may jeo-pardize her self-esteem, her residency status, her job, and her rela-tionships with family and community. Under the circumstances, it is not surprising that many Latinas prefer to remain silent. Never-theless, the experience of the East Los Angeles Rape Hotline con-firms that this population can be reached through the usual means of making services known. Word of mouth and agency referrals seem to generate the largest number of calls. Routine posting of flyers in churches, in community agencies, and in community places of business has also proved effective.

Attracting the Latina client, however, is but the beginning of offering acceptable care. While the description which has been given of Latino attitudes toward rape has many counterparts in other cultures, caregivers must take into account numerous special factors which may influence both survivor and caretaker. The guidelines below summarize some of the experience of the East Los Angeles Hotline workers.

Some General Guidelines

1. Caregivers, whether of Latino or non-Latino origin, must examine their attitudes for stereotypical views of Latinas and

Latina survivors. Traditional biases which may linger in the consciousness of Latina caregivers can lead to further abuse of the survivor, as can myths about Latinas prevalent in Anglo-American culture. Ignorance, prejudice, and racism in the Anglo-American society oppress Latinos in general, and Latinas in particular. Anglo stereotypes of Latinas as uneducated, intellectually inferior, unsophisticated, overly dependent, masochistic, or eager for sex are common and are difficult to overcome without conscious effort.

The Latina may be at any point in the spectrum from very recent immigration to various degrees of acculturation in American mainstream values. Caregivers must determine the particular situation of the survivor and take it into consideration.

2. Caregivers must assure the availability of bilingual services for Latinas who are mainly Spanish-speaking. Because of the Spanish-speaking person's fear of being viewed as one of lower status, a Latina may claim that she is capable of working with an English-speaking person. In her desire to be treated more positively, she may state that she is bilingual when, in fact, she may be limited in the expression of feelings in her second language. It is important to note that affective expression is always more readily accessible in one's native language.

It is also important to consider the educational level of the survivor and that of her family and friends. Language skills and reading skills may vary widely. Written materials should be designed with the advice of those who are familiar with the socio-economic levels of the predominant Latino community of a particular area. Assumptions should not be made, and care must be taken to protect the dignity of the individual, regardless of formal education. The knowledge and practice of courtesy and respect for others, which Latinos also regard as a mark of education, are generally considered important by Latinos from every walk of life.

3. The immigrant Latina whose legal status in the country is a concern must not be further abused by denial of sensitive assistance or by threats of deportation or loss of her job. Caregivers' willingness to intervene effectively, regardless of her status, and to hold the assailant accountable, will contribute to the survivor's well-being and to the decrease of exploitation of immigrant Latinas.

4. The Latina experiences the same emotional reactions to

sexual assault as any woman. In addition, the Latina who feels that her past or present behavior provoked the assault, and that she has committed a sin, may be struggling with both traditional religious values and American myths. She may need help to understand the reality of sexual assault as violence, not sex; that women do not provoke it; and that any woman, regardless of her behavior, may become the victim of rape.

The Latina survivor may feel guilty, as well as particularly concerned about being violated, "soiled," or no longer a virgin. The possibility or actuality of venereal disease resulting from the assault may aggravate these feelings. Feelings of guilt may be heightened further if the victim did not resist. Religious stories abound of women who became saints when they preferred death to the loss of their virginity. Caregivers with sensitivity to the cultural and religious implications of sexual assault for the Latina can assist her to deal with rape as violence, rather than sex. It is useful to point out that giving up virginity is an autonomous act. Religious authorities—priests, nuns, ministers, rabbis—can assist the Latina and her family with reassurances appropriate to their particular beliefs.

5. Because of taboos surrounding any subject that is viewed as sexual, it may be difficult for the Latina to acknowledge various assaultive acts she may have been forced to endure. In addition, words that adequately describe such acts and body parts may not be in the routine vocabulary of the Latina whose primary language is not English. Caregivers who understand Latino values and mores and who can appropriately discuss the acts and body parts in the language of the survivor are particularly helpful.

6. Concern about pregnancy resulting from the assault and about alternate ways of dealing with it may be great for Latinas who do not believe in artificial birth control or abortion. Some rape survivors may choose to keep their babies should pregnancy occur, or even, in some cases, to marry the rapist. Such choices are influenced by the conviction that once a woman is no longer a virgin, her chances for a good marriage are limited or non-existent. Caregivers must be prepared to help the victim arrive in her own way at the resolution that seems most appropriate to her. For the young Latina, especially, the enlistment of family support for her decision may be important.

7. Gang rapes and individual sexual assaults perpetrated by men in positions of authority over Latinas have been identified as a particular problem in some cities. The emotional impact of a brutal assault by multiple assailants is likely to be especially crisis producing. The Latina survivor of gang rape may be fearful of reprisal by gang members if she seeks assistance. Also, the discovery of gang rape carries the threat of "spreading the word" that the victim was a willing subject, thereby deepening her anxiety about her reputation and her chances of marriage to a "good" man. Caregivers may need to emphasize the responsibility and the accountability of assailants, not victims, for the crime of rape.

8. The Latina may be fearful of serious family repercussions if she discloses the sexual assault. Many Latino families instill in their children the principle of "protecting" the name and honor of the family. Discussion of intimate problems with outsiders is regarded as a violation of the sanctity of the home. Thus, the family may look upon the survivor as a traitor if she discloses anything viewed as so intimate a matter as rape. It is therefore essential to reassure regarding the issue of confidentiality. It is equally important to discuss the psychological benefits to be derived from talking out one's feelings.

9. There is also the possibility that the entire family may feel that its honor has been violated by the assault. The Latina may fear that her male relatives will seek revenge through violence against the assailant, further aggravating the family's situation. Caregivers aware of traditional Latino values may need to offer the family and significant others assistance in dealing with their feelings in a way that upholds their dignity and, at the same time, is non-destructive and supportive of the survivor. It is helpful to stress that the strength of the family, if channelled into support of the survivor, can make an important contribution to a positive resolution of the assault.

10. If the Latina has been socialized to feel that the externalization of anger is unacceptable, she may need assistance in dealing with the anger provoked by sexual assault. Caregivers may need to assure the Latina survivor that her anger is a normal reaction, which can be expressed in non-self-destructive ways.

11. Caregivers must be well informed about a variety of referral resources, particularly those offering bilingual/bicultural

services, to meet the survivor's needs. In addition to offering Spanish language services, referral agencies need to be sensitive to the specific concerns of the client which arise from traditional cultural values.

12.   Caregivers who are not familiar with the specific cultural factors which influence a Latina's reactions to sexual assault can avoid being perceived as insensitive through an attitude of respect and validation for her feelings and beliefs. The Latina, in general, and the foreign-born Latina in particular, may fear invalidation and negation of her cultural identity by Anglo-Americans. Asking for information needed to understand the victim's needs and feelings demonstrates the caregiver's concern and respect. It is of utmost importance to maintain a non-judgmental and accepting manner at all times.

Making Choices: A Final Word

As we have already observed, many Latinas, particularly adolescents, have strong feelings of respect for authority. While these feelings are generally directed toward family members, some clients may turn to the counselor as the figure in authority. In these cases, special care must be exercised to offer information and guidance, while firmly returning decision-making power to the client. Survivors may require repeated reassurances of their ability to make their own choices and to live with the consequences. In this connection, as in all other aspects of treatment, respect for the survivor, taking into consideration her individuality as well as her particular cultural circumstances, provides the key to effective care.

NOTES

1.   The term "survivor" was introduced in California by the State Coalition of Rape Crisis Centers.

2.   We use *Latino* (feminine, *Latina*) as a universal term encompassing Chicanos, Mexican-Americans, Mexicans, Central Americans, South Americans, Puerto Ricans, and Cubans, in preference to *Hispano/ Hispana*, which suggests white ancestry rather than the Indian ancestry of

most of the population of Latin America. We use the more specific *Chicano/Chicana* for Spanish-speaking persons of Indian heritage reared in the United States.

3. *Hombre*, referring to one who is a man, in contrast to *macho*, referring to a male animal and carrying connotations of brutality, especially in attitudes and behavior demeaning to women.

4. The Hotline attributes the high incidence of callers in this age group to several factors: (1) many referrals by schools, churches, and other community agencies which service youth; (2) greater readiness of young women to ask for help because of their "loss," as compared to adult women who may accept the view of themselves as having "nothing to lose"; (3) the more urgent need of the youthful woman to get outside support when she fears or feels rejected by adults who are normally her main support.

5. John M. MacDonald, *Rape Offenders and Their Victims* (Springfield, Ill.: Charles C. Thomas Publishing Company, 1979). Studies such as MacDonald's, based on convicted rapists only, are considered inconclusive due to the low percentage of rapists who actually receive convictions.

The Second Mile: New Directions for Young Women

Sue Davidson

New Directions for Young Women, Tucson, Arizona, was founded in 1976, with the assistance of a grant from the Office of Juvenile Justice and Delinquency Prevention.[1] While its cost-free services are available to any female between the ages of twelve and twenty-one, a central goal of New Directions has been to provide alternatives to incarceration for young women involved in the juvenile justice system. Like other adolescents, these young women experience many difficulties as they move into adulthood. Their problems may include an inability to communicate with their parents, lack of sex and health information, lack of job skills, and the social and economic consequences of running away from home. Although such problems may be common to males and females, young women also encounter special difficulties because of their sex. They are more often victims of physical and sexual abuse; they may be unable to attend school because of pregnancy or child-rearing responsibilities; as a result of sex-role stereotyping, they may have very limited views of their choices and of their potential abilities. In the case of low-income young women, particularly,

Much of the material for this article was gathered from the staff of New Directions for Young Women. The author is grateful for the assistance of these women: Barbara Chana, Hollis Heming-way, Pat Osborn, Debby Rosenberg, and Betsy Steele, of the counseling staff; Ruth Crow, executive director of the agency's National Female Advocacy Project; Carol Zimmerman, executive director of New Directions; Linda Kegerreis, former assistant director.

49

conflicts with their families or at school may lead to involvement with police and courts. The juvenile court is often used as a "solution" for "unruly girls" whose economic position puts other resources out of reach.

New Directions set out to perform two principle functions: (1) to provide direct services to individual young women; (2) to advocate for needed changes in the institutions which affect young women as a class—schools, courts, health and welfare agencies. In New Directions' philosophy, direct services and advocacy are intimately related. For while improved direct services are an end in themselves, they cannot solve the complex social and political problems which affect the rights and welfare of young women. These problems must be attacked through institutional change. At the same time, it is daily contact with young women and first-hand familiarity with the institutions bearing on their lives which provide the needed "reality base" for effective advocacy. In short, each of these efforts—social services and social action—nourishes and informs the other.

Counselors and Counseling Approach

New Directions counselors have come from a variety of class, racial, and educational backgrounds. Racial composition of the counseling staff, over the years, has corresponded roughly to the usual ethnic distribution of clients: 56 percent Caucasian; 30 percent Mexican American; 10 percent Native American; 4 percent Black. Counselors who are women of color have been especially valuable as role models for clients, as well as for their extensive contacts within their own communities. The staff has included women with graduate degrees, trained in counseling, teaching, and other fields, and women with some years of undergraduate education or high school degrees, who have previously worked in programs serving youth, women, or minorities.

More important for New Directions counselors than any specific preparation, perhaps, are commitment and perseverance. They must be willing to walk the proverbial second mile with clients who may hesitate to take any steps at all, since their experiences have given them few reasons to trust the world, the counselor, or themselves. By the time clients arrive at New Directions' doors, they have usually been through many other doors—among them, foster homes, group homes, runaway shelters, juvenile detention centers, state prisons for girls, and mental institutions. A listing of their typical problems includes family violence, conflicts with families, incest, rape, school dropout, homelessness, unintended pregnancy, single parenthood, unemployment and/or lack of training.

There is little in the experience of these young women which can give them a positive self-image and the sense that they can gain control even over their own bodies, much less their lives. New Directions aims at increasing the actual competency of these young women, at the same time cultivating their feelings of self-worth. Informational and skills-building programs, as well as individual and group counseling, are means which contribute to these aims.

In developing its counseling approaches, New Directions looked to the feminist movement of the 1970s, adapting the insights of consciousness-raising and feminist therapy to fit the needs of adolescents. Some principles which have emerged may be summarized as follows:

1. The counselor helps the client to distinguish between the person she is and the roles imposed upon her by social conditioning. In assisting the client to define herself for herself, she helps to free her from limiting or demeaning stereotypes.

2. The counselor seeks a mutually respectful, non-authoritarian relationship with the client. Openness about her own values and attitudes helps to decrease the distance and equalize the relationship between herself and the client.

3. The client is the person who knows most about her own thoughts and feelings; in this matter, she is the "expert" in the counseling situation. The primary function of the counselor is to offer emotional support, as well as information and guidance about the adult world.

4. As a model for young women, the counselor demonstrates that it is possible to be assertive and capable at the same time that one is sensitive and understanding. The counselor can serve the client best as a model if the client perceives that, as women, they share common experiences.

5. The counselor encourages the client to form bonds with adolescent and adult women and to seek support from them. The all-female group is particularly valuable toward this end. Distinct

social experiences of women which lead to individual feelings of powerlessness—from rape to sexual jokes and innuendo—can be dealt with most effectively in the all-female group. The group model enables young women to: (a) recognize that their problems are not peculiar to themselves; (b) identify and validate each other's strengths; (c) break down their isolation; (d) help each other perceive a variety of responses which can be made to issues arising in daily female experience.

Like a number of contemporary therapies, New Directions counseling departs from the traditional medical model, which locates the source of conflicts within individuals, with no reference to the social and economic systems impinging upon their lives. The inequities characteristic of these systems, the effects of gender, race, class, and sexual orientation, account for many of the conflicts of New Directions' clients, their feelings of inadequacy, their low self-esteem. In addition, it is common for adolescent women— especially those have been labeled "offenders"—to see themselves as "bad," "crazy," "weird," or intrinsically inferior. By rejecting an orientation in which the young woman is viewed as "sick," the counselor demonstrates respect for the client, encouraging her to see herself as a person capable of taking charge of many aspects of her life.

Consistent with its non-traditional counseling approach, New Directions has evolved a flexible work style to accommodate its clients' needs. It is need, rather than agency convenience, which determines over how long a period of time a client will be seen, how much time is given to a meeting with a client, and how the time is spent. The fifty-minute office hour of traditional therapy is seldom suitable for New Directions clientele. In fact, counselors are more often with clients away from the office than in it:

"The kids just turn up on the doorstep of my house."

"For a while, she was getting into a lot of fights at school; the school counselors would call, and I'd go right down."

"She'd been depressed, and when she didn't show for her appointment, I was worried. She and her friends usually go to Jack-in-the-Box after school, so I started out looking for her there."

"I can see a young woman's whole family if I go to her house at night. They're more accessible at home and also feel more comfortable."

"I hadn't heard from her for weeks, and then around two o'clock one morning, her husband punched her and walked out, so she telephoned, and I went over."

Clearly, New Directions counselors often do not have the advantage of controlling the environment in which counseling takes place. Such a situation would not suit service providers who prefer that meetings take place on their own territory, in some regular and regulated fashion. But New Directions' style has certain definite advantages. Willingness to be flexible often makes the difference between keeping in contact with a client and losing her. Further, the client is frequently seen with friends and family members, in many different settings and situations which are relevant to *her* life. Thus, the counselor is able to observe and learn much more about her than is possible in meetings and activities confined within the agency.

Programs offered at the agency, for that matter, do not invariably give the appearance of being "regular" or "regulated." Members of the young mothers' support group, for example, often bring their toddlers to the meetings—understandably, since many participants are unable to make child care arrangements. "The young mothers will often turn up early, or straggle in late," reports the agency's director. "They bring their children into the main office, and the toddlers crawl and climb around, 'interrupting' our work. Well, it's not an 'interruption.' Although it may look sloppy to an outsider, it *is* our work."

Groups: Information, Training, Mutual Support

Groups at New Directions may arise from interests directly expressed by young women or from the needs they express indirectly. "Assertion training" is a term that New Directions clients, in general, are probably not familiar with before they visit the agency, but it answers to an almost universal need among them. As females, they have been socialized to keep quietly in the background, not to express their views, not to initiate action. These social messages do not serve them well as they make the transition from adolescence to adulthood. Adult responsibility requires women to define clearly what they want and to know how to ask for it, as well as how to reject what they do not want.

The first lesson in the training is designed to teach young

women the difference between passive, assertive, and aggressive behavior. Once a young woman understands these distinctions, she is encouraged to experiment with assertive behavior within the safety of the group by speaking up for herself in a strong but not hostile manner and by expressing her needs without discounting those of others. With good reason, she may be fearful of expressing herself assertively, because others, especially male authority figures, may let her know that it is "unbecoming" to her and threatening to them. In practicing assertive behavior, she has an opportunity to learn, perhaps for the first time, how it feels to stand up for herself without being hostile and to gain some perspective on how to deal with negative reactions. Role-playing a variety of responses to several simulated situations, she is able to compare the probable consequences of being assertive with the results of passive or aggressive behavior. This enables her to make informed decisions about whether, and under what circumstances, she wishes to be assertive. Having the knowledge that she can make a choice about her behavior helps a young woman to increase awareness of her strengths and to build her self-confidence.

New Directions clients ask both directly and in indirect ways for sexual information. New Directions regularly offers classes on sexuality, both at the agency and through the public schools and other cooperating community agencies. "Our Bodies, Ourselves," based on the book of that title, was one of the first courses designed by New Directions.[2] Its goal is to promote informed choice. The series of meetings begins with a discussion of how young women participants feel about themselves as females. It is another opportunity to realize that many of their feelings are shared by their peers, and that insight and information are the first steps toward taking control. Topics include the Anatomy and Physiology of Sexuality, Reproduction, Responsible Sexuality, Birth Control, Pregnancy, and Available Health Care Resources. Each of these subjects is discussed with the aim of dispelling myths and misconceptions.

The sexual repression that has been historically visited upon women and youth is currently combined with the sexual freedom, "do-your-thing" message from the "hip" 1960s. Young women are often caught in the middle of this double message. Some of them reject traditional prohibitions against any sexual activity outside of marriage, only to respond to contemporary cultural pressures to have sex with anyone who asks. The sexuality groups provide a young woman with the emotional support and the necessary information to make her own decisions about her sexual life, according to her own personal values.

Attitudes about sexuality may vary widely from one culture to another. A special group on sexuality, designed by a Pima-Papago staff member and limited to Native American participants, recently drew not only adolescent women, but their mothers and grandmothers.

Teenagers who become pregnant are more than half as likely to drop out of school as other young women.[3] New Directions introduces teen mothers, mothers-to-be, and other young women to community programs in which they are tutored for a high school equivalency examination, leading to the General Education Degree (G.E.D.). New Directions' own G.E.D. program has combined the tutorial course with a course in job acquisition and consumer education. Although the program has been discontinued because of a shortage of funds, it provides a model for motivating young women, who can better appreciate the value of a high school degree as it relates to becoming self-supporting and living independently.

Other New Directions courses have included Career Awareness, Life Planning, and Values Clarification. Designed with sensitivity to the situation of young women, these more "usual" courses take on new significance. More "unusual" courses, such as Assertion Training, are frequently redesigned to fit the needs of special populations, such as disabled young women.

Advocacy: Activity on Many Fronts

Much of the work of New Directions counselors is in case advocacy. A counselor may act as an advocate for a client within the client's family, helping her to negotiate an agreement which can resolve conflicts. She may be the client's advocate with health or welfare agencies, assisting her with bureaucratic red tape. Often, counselors act as mediators to keep clients in school or in such training and employment programs as the Job Corps, when conflicts develop.

As is obvious from these examples, counselors do not maintain a position of neutrality when clients come into conflict with individuals or systems that may be vital to their interests. They do not always accept their clients' views of such conflicts, but they consider it important to support them in any positive effort they may make, such as sticking to a jobs program, attending to their health needs, or staying in school. Recognizing that their clients are at a disadvantage not only socially and economically, but also as females and as young persons with few legal and personal rights, they will "go to bat" for them. One counselor observes:

> We try to teach them how to deal with systems that might otherwise overwhelm them. When we go as their advocates, to intervene for them in the courts, in schools, at health care agencies, we're deliberately giving them lessons in how to do it for themselves. We're trying to prepare them to deal with the kinds of situations they'll most likely need to cope with all their lives.
>
> We also try to give them every bit of information that might expand their opportunities. We encourage them to take the G.E.D., if they can't or won't stay in school. We've worked at increasing the options available to them, as, for example, in non-traditional jobs for women. Of course, right now, the options are shrinking. We don't ignore the realities. When a young woman says, in effect, that the system doesn't value her, we say, you're right, it doesn't—but you have the choice of getting all the information you can, and using it to your benefit, to at least try to get what you want. We encourage them to take risks, even it that sometimes means failure. We let them know that's a learning experience—they can take that failure to us, and we examine it together, and they learn from it. If only by a little bit, and a little bit at a time, they can learn ways of increasing their power and self-respect, in spite of how society may regard them.

Encouraging young women to exercise power, to strive for self-determination, to refuse to be victims, at the same time that they must survive in a world which prefers complaisant females, is a difficult tightrope act. In the case of New Directions clients, there is the continuing possibility that a mis-step will lead the client back into the juvenile justice system. New Directions counselors might be tempted to "save" young women—either by suggesting that they conform to traditional expectations of female passivity, or, using the power inherent in the counseling relationship, by making "best" decisions for the client. Since their convictions and their counseling philosophy make these routes impossible, they redouble their efforts, their attention, their time, and their support, going the second mile with clients who have few or no other places to turn for sympathetic, non-coercive assistance.

The "second mile" extends beyond individual clients and into the community, where New Directions' effort is to influence institutions and agencies in ways that will improve the conditions and opportunities of young women. Few services exist for female youth in any community, relative to those available to young males.[4] Virtually all youth services and programs, other than those of the traditional girl-serving agencies, such as the Y.W.C.A. and Girl Scouts, are male-oriented, including those that purportedly serve both sexes. Further, the attitudes and practices of many counselors,mental health personnel, and juvenile court workers have a negative impact on young women, particularly those young women who fail to conform to socially approved "feminine" behavior: docility, uncritical obedience to parental and school authority, sexual modesty. Young women who rebel against the limitations of the traditional female role are often "treated" to improve their "mental health." Meanwhile, the real needs of adolescent women go unattended.

New Directions has raised the issue of young women's needs through an aggressive program of public education and through cultivating the cooperation of a broad range of private and governmental agencies. A forum co-sponsored with the Arizona Women's Commission, for example, brought together high level state policy makers to hear recommendations for policy reforms affecting teenage female employment, family relations, and juvenile court practices. A New Directions conference on "Sexuality and Socialization" focused on Mexican American cultural attitudes toward sexuality as these affect adolescent women. La Frontera Center, a Tucson agency, and Planned Parenthood of Southern Arizona co-sponsored this unusual event. Training in areas ranging from sex-role stereotyping to sexual molestation is regularly offered by New Directions to teachers, counselors, juvenile justice personnel, and the personnel of health, social service, and employment agencies. Lesbian adolescence was the subject of a training session attended by youth workers from the Arizona State Department of Corrections and county juvenile court staff. New Directions has also provided impetus and assistance for the creation of new programs benefitting adolescent women. One of its early successes was a collaborative project with the Y.W.C.A. and the Tucson Urban League which provided work experience for young women in non-traditional jobs. Occasionally, New Directions takes to the streets to call attention to key concerns. For several years, staff members have been central organizers in the "Take Back the Night" marches protesting rape, and have joined other supporters in marching for equal rights and protesting day care funding cuts.

In its relatively brief history, New Directions has built good working relationships with the many agencies with which it exchanges program information and referrals; and it has had an impact on more than a few of them. But while New Directions has a "good image" in the community, its work of advocacy is not without tensions. Its stance is, after all, critical of things-as-they-are; its change objectives necessarily cause discomfort among those who are asked to accommodate and forward change. An official of the Pima County Juvenile Court, Tucson, described the interaction between the court and New Directions, in the words of Martin Luther King, Jr., as one of "creative conflict." To chance conflict on a continuing basis, intervening in the systems and with the persons affecting young women's lives, is not a job that everyone would relish. But New Directions staff—which has been a remarkably stable one—appears to welcome the challenge. As one counselor said, with deliberate inelegance: "We're just sorry that we don't have the time to hustle more territories."

Much of the stamina at New Directions arises from the close and supportive relationships among staff, particularly among counselors, who say that they feel "like a family." This has not, however, happened by chance. In their consultations with one another on cases, in their planning of agency programs, in their division of responsibilities, in their identification of inevitable irritations and differences, "we've worked hard on how we work together," a counselor remarks. Another adds, "We've had to. You really couldn't do this job alone."

Afterword: Trina W.
A Counselor Describes a Case

I'm going to talk about a client I've been seeing, on and off, for the past three years. I'll call her Trina W. I first met her when she was twelve years old. She was well grown for her age, and in good health. She was referred to New Directions by the juvenile court, where she'd been charged with running away from home, ditching school and fighting at school, and smoking grass.

Although Trina has been my primary client, I've worked with all the members of the family—the mother and father, three sisters, three brothers, an aunt, and some cousins. It's a welfare family. The parents are separated. Both are alcoholics. The children live with their mother; their father turns up periodically. The mother is usually unemployed, has no money, is in poor health. She cares about her children, but can't cope with that large family. The violence in the family is a major problem for Trina. It isn't directed at her, but there are drinking bouts in which the mother and father fight with each other, and the brothers fight each other. Part of my work with Trina was in helping her find shelter when, during these family brawls, they would kick her out of the house in the middle of the night.

Trina was extremely cooperative from the time I first met her, although she was very shy. It took a while for her to talk easily with me. Almost immediately, however, she confided to me that she thought she might be pregnant, and when I took her to Planned Parenthood, her suspicion was confirmed. There was a boyfriend, and it was an initial exploration, a first intercourse, from which she became pregnant. The mother was very angry, and Trina was subject to a lot of verbal abuse. Eventually, both Trina's mother and father agreed with her that she should have an abortion, but they were not willing to go through that with her. So I went through it with her, and it was very difficult. She had some abortion counseling at Planned Parenthood, which lasted a long time. Eventually, she was able to talk about it, talk about how she felt, and also about her boyfriend.

The ditching of school, fighting, the pot smoking—from the time I started working with her, those things have stopped. The running away from home has not stopped, but she doesn't do that except when it's entirely appropriate. She simply leaves home when things get rough, and she goes and stays with a friend or a relative, and goes back, after it's over. It's not called running away when she does it now; it's not reported to the courts. Her probation was dismissed, because she's been in no further trouble with the court.

Much of my work with Trina has simply been support, advocacy, and giving her a sense of what happens in the world. A lot of it is assuring her that *she's* O.K., and that the crazy things in her life *are* crazy, and that they're not her fault, and that she has a lot of survival skills. She survived to the age of twelve very well. We've talked a lot about what happens when the family fights, and what she can do to take care of herself. She cares a lot about her family, and it's very hard for her; she can get involved in the fighting, if only because she's trying to hold somebody back to keep them from hurting each other. She now has a very good sense of the drinking and fighting cycles, the signs of when something's going to happen, and she just clears out. I have, of course, given her a lot of information about other options. We've talked about Child Protective Services, and the choice she has of living with another family, but she has no desire to do that. She feels that to go to a foster home, with an environment that might be completely different than the one she's accustomed to, would be more terrifying than staying in her own home, where at least she knows what's happening.

Trina is a very bright young woman. She did want to go to school, she did want help. Now she has an excellent attendance record. Her grades are good, even though she has a hard time studying at home because of the family situation. She gets absolutely no support from her family for being in school—in fact, they harrass her for it. Initially her self-confidence was very low. We've done a lot of work on that, we've talked about her skills, and how she does have choices. She's very talented in sports and is naturally athletic, but had been doing nothing in those areas. A couple of years ago, the school coach had wanted her to be on the track team, and she had said no. But after a while, with some encouragement, she made up her mind to do it.

So now she's on the track team, she's on a summer softball team, and she's getting very involved in tennis at school. Her family gives her no praise for any of these activities—they never go to see her play. But we've worked on building up her support systems. When I first met her, she didn't have many friends, she kept mostly to herself. The only person she really cared about was her boyfriend, and once she got pregnant, she was forbidden to see him again, which was devastating to her. Now she's talking more to kids at school. She has more friends, people she can go to stay with, when she needs to do that.

I've given her a lot of information on what's possible for her with respect to employment and education. At some point, I'd say nine months ago, she finally said that maybe she thought she'd like to go to college and to be a teacher of physical education. I believe that she can do that, with some encouragement, and she's beginning to believe that she can do that, as well. She many change her mind about going to college or what work she'd like—she's only fifteen. But whatever she decides, I think she now has a sense that she can do it.

I've done continuing work with Trina's family. I did pregnancy counseling with her sister, also working with the mother—showed them films, talked about childbirth, gave them information. When one of Trina's brothers was in trouble, her mother requested that I work with him. I've also helped the mother at certain times when she has been under high stress.

I've also done some crisis counseling with Trina, when there was fighting. We've talked a lot about what it means to be assertive in that situation—although I don't use those words with her. It means that she can say no, she can divorce herself from that part of the family situation. They may be angry with her, but probably not much angrier than they already are. There were a couple of times when Trina felt suicidal. Other times she's been very depressed, although less frequently in the last six to nine months. We have talked a lot about what she can do about her depression. Because she's a very physical person, physical activity like running helps her—just getting away from the house and doing something active. When she's been depressed, it has been important for her to have somebody she can talk to, even though it's hard for her to talk. I would say that she is no longer suicidal. She's in a lot better place than she used to be. However, as long as she remains in the family, some of those dangers remain. And it is her choice to stay in the family.

One of the things that we do in groups at New Directions is to offer young women some new experiences. I've done a lot of that with Trina, because I know she's one of my clients who will profit most from that. Things like taking her to the ballet, to sporting events, hiking, to the circus, the museum. I encourage her to go or take her myself, because those are experiences that otherwise she would not have, and she really does enjoy them.

We've had a lot of discussions about sexuality. There've been a lot of pregnancies in Trina's family, and although the brothers can go out and become fathers, there's a premium on women not getting pregnant. Trina is very much aware of the possibilities of pregnancy. We have talked about birth control. She's decided that while she wanted to be with her boyfriend, because she needed a friend, someone she could be close to, that's not something she wants for herself right now, and she's watching, she's just being careful. She has friends, but she's not being sexually active at this time. And she says she will use birth control, if she does decide to be sexually active.

I want to make it clear that all along Trina has been making her own decisions. I have not made them for her. For instance, when she discovered that she was pregnant, and we discussed all the different options, and the dangers, and the possibilities, it was Trina's decision to have an abortion.

Trina is the kind of client that it's really satisfying to work with. She's smart and she picks up things well. All she really wanted and needed was someone to give her some support and information, a little extra help, and I've been able to do that.

At this time, I think my work with Trina is pretty much done. We stay in touch. She always knows that she can call me, and she does that sometimes. I'm someone she knows she can rely on.

I feel good about the changes Trina has made since I've known her. But I think that without me, she still would have made changes. I believe it would have been much more difficult for her. I know that I've been an important person in her life. Now I can step back. But there is still a strong affection. . . . I care a whole lot about her.

NOTES

1. The agency is also funded by grants from private foundations and by United Way of Tucson, the City of Tucson, and private donations.

2. Boston Women's Health Collective, *Our Bodies, Ourselves* (New York: Simon and Schuster, 1977).

3. The Alan Guttmacher Institute, *Teenage Pregnancy: The Problem That Hasn't Gone Away* (New York, 1981), p. 30.

4. The low priority placed on serving young women is evident in funding patterns. A mid-1970s report revealed that "girls organizations receive only $1.00 out of every $4.00 that corporate foundations donate to youth agencies." Girls Clubs of America, Inc., broadside, "Agencies Serving Girls Can No Longer Operate Efficiently with a Stove, a Sewing Machine and a Loving Heart," incorporating breakdown of United Way allocations in 1976 (N.d.). Studies have also documented glaring diparities in public funds allocated to programs for young women and young men; for example, from 1969 to 1975, only 5 percent of all federally-funded projects in juvenile justice were specifically earmarked for females, while the local expenditure of juvenile justice funds on programs for young women was only 6 percent. Law Enforcement Assistance Administration, *The Report of the LEAA Task Force on Women*, October 1, 1975, p. 10. Currently, the budget offered by the Reagan Administration slashes all programs of special assistance to young women, in education, training and jobs, and human resources.

Teenage Street Women:
A Group Counseling Model

Elaine D. Schroeder

Introduction

In 1981 and 1982 I led a research project to develop and evaluate a counseling program for teenage street women, who are part of a growing population of street prostitutes.[1] The group counseling model described here grew out of my clinical and field work experience in Seattle, Washington, with young prostitutes and other young women who were delinquent or who had run away. I established contacts with this population both in a juvenile detention facility and on the streets where young prostitutes gather.

During street-based field work, I was assisted by an outreach worker from a local youth shelter[2] and an eighteen-year-old prostitute. These women—one of them, like myself, a Caucasian, one of them a Chicana—also participated as assistants in leading the group sessions described in this paper. For approximately seven months, our team met with and interviewed young female prostitutes who worked the downtown Seattle prostitution locale. A snack shop in this area was a popular meeting place for run-aways, young male and female prostitutes, and occasionally pimps. We found the snack shop a good place to meet and chat informally with young street women. We were able to assist some of them to find housing or health care while we were in the process of developing the counseling model.

After establishing trust and rapport with a number of street women, we invited some of them to join us for weekly informal discussion sessions in a nearby office or at a restaurant. These small group meetings were planned to test the feasibility of holding weekly scheduled counseling groups. Despite efforts to arrange these sessions at times when young street women were free, the weekly meetings were poorly attended.[3] Individual appointments we made with young prostitutes were also rarely kept. This was the case even though many young women said they wanted to meet with us. Those who missed sessions commonly explained that they had been sick, had overslept, or had taken too many drugs; others may have been jailed. A few young women indicated that their pimps or boyfriends had discouraged them from coming. We eventually decided to work only with young women who were not with a pimp, because of the danger to them and to us of street violence if their pimps should object to their participation in our project.[4]

Difficulties in attempting to organize regular meetings with young women have been reported by other programs for juvenile prostitutes. For example, Project S.T.A.R.T., a Seattle program for juvenile prostitutes, is primarily outreach-focused because the most reliable method of contacting clients is through spontaneous encounters on the streets.

Form, Settings, and Participants

Our experience with the young prostitutes we met on the streets led to the design of an intensive three-day counseling program which required only one initial commitment by the participant. The fast turnover of the prisoners we contacted in detention also pointed to the need for an intervention that was brief, but intensive.

A total of twenty-four young women between the ages of thirteen and eighteen participated in the three counseling groups we conducted. Two of our groups met in a juvenile detention facility; the third, composed of young women we had contacted in the downtown prostitution locale, met in a private setting outside the city. There were five to eight participants in each group. While most of our participants in detention were black, the young prostitutes we contacted in the downtown prostitution locale were mainly white. Apparently young black prostitutes solicited in another part of town.

Like female adolescent prostitutes described in studies con-

ducted in Minneapolis[5] and Seattle,[6] the majority of our participants came from disrupted and abusive families, were school drop-
outs, and had a history of running away. Most came from poor
families.

Family relations. Sixteen of our twenty-four participants were
not living at home prior to volunteering for the counseling program. Twenty-one of our participants had run away from home at
some time; eight of these had run away over ten times.

Abuse. Most of the participants in our program reported that
they had suffered from sexual and other physical abuse at home.
Two-thirds of the Minneapolis study's female adolescent prostitutes had been beaten by a family member, and 31 percent
reported sexual abuse by a family member.[7]

School and arrests. Street youths have usually dropped out of
school, and many have been arrested for prostitution or other
crimes. Participants in our counseling program were an average of
approximately two years behind the grade level appropriate for
their age. All but one of our twenty-four participants had been arrested; ten had been arrested more than five times. Many young
prostitutes become involved in other criminal activities, especially
theft and drug trade.

Consequences of Prostitution Lifestyle

The consequences of prostitution as a lifestyle for adolescents
are overwhelmingly negative. Street violence is an everpresent
threat. A number of the young women we interviewed told us
about beatings by pimps and customers; and at least one of the
young women in our program was later murdered. Poor nutrition,
irregular meals and sleep schedules, and insufficiency of medical
care add to the health hazards on the streets. While we cannot
predict the future of young prostitutes when and if they become
adults, it is likely that their choice of occupations outside of prostitution or other illegal activities will be limited. Many will not return
to school or have access to other training leading to "straight"
jobs. The probability of young street women forming healthy relationships and establishing stable family lives may be diminished
because so many had abusive and inadequate parents and subsequently lacked positive role models. Sexually abused and battered
children are likely to suffer developmentally and to be psycho-

socially at risk as adults.[8]

Programs for Adolescent Prostitutes

Although juvenile prostitution is a rapidly growing social problem, it has only recently been recognized by the public and by social agencies. Just a handful of residential and outreach programs are specifically designed to serve this population.[9] Despite their energetic efforts, the problem of juvenile prostitution is too great to be affected by a few programs, even assuming their effectiveness. There has, however, been no systematic attempt to test the effectiveness of various interventions for this population.

Intervention Goals

In selecting goals for our intervention with adolescent prostitutes, it was important to consider certain underlying causes of this social problem. Although family disruption, sexual abuse, and neglect are often antecedents of juvenile prostitution, they are catalysts, rather than basic causes. The feminist analysis guiding this intervention views juvenile prostitution as the product of a social system in which gender is the primary basis of social status and power, and in which women are defined largely by their sexuality.[10] Consent to basic sexist (patriarchal) values is obtained primarily through the socialization of both men and women regarding temperament, role, and status. Women are defined as docile, dependent, and possessing less urgent sexual needs than males. In fact, prostitution is commonly understood to exist for the purpose of servicing the supposedly imperious sexual drive of males. Prostitution is supported by a prevailing double standard which permits far greater freedom in sexual behavior for males than for females.

Traditional criminologists have often viewed prostitution as an individual pathology,[11] and well-meaning social workers have implied the same.[12] This reliance on a pathology model serves to blame the victim while it legitimizes the status quo of incarcerating and punishing the young prostitute. The counseling program described here focused on immediate assistance to adolescent prostitutes and other young women at risk. It was undergirded by recognition that counseling alone will not solve the problem of juvenile prostitution.

Global vs. Limited Goals

Many social service providers who work with young prostitutes expect that as a result of their help, their clients will leave the streets. This is an unrealistic expectation, inasmuch as young prostitute clients rarely return for a second appointment, and even fewer leave the streets permanently as the direct result of counseling. Prostituting is not an isolated activity; it is part of a total lifestyle. When young women begin to solicit on the streets, they are changing their entire way of living, including how they view themselves, and how others view them.

In a comprehensive study of delinquency interventions, Dennis Romig concludes that while most treatment for delinquent youth has little effect, a promising treatment approach is a behavioral one, with limited, specific objectives.[13] For our own intervention, we sought intermediate goals—those which, if met, might enable young women to make their own decisions and act upon them. A synthesis of what young street women stated they needed in a counseling group, what we discovered through clinical and field contacts, and what we had learned from the literature on prostitution was the basis of our ultimate selection of specific primary and secondary goals.

Primary and Secondary Goals of the Counseling Model

The primary goal of our intervention was to increase the self-esteem of participants. The three secondary goals were to improve problem-solving skills, increase women's health knowledge, and encourage positive female relationships. Each of these goals is discussed below..

Goal one: increase self-esteem. Young prostitutes, both in descriptive studies and in our program, overwhelmingly appear to suffer from low self-esteem, especially that arising from negative sexual labeling. Self-esteem is an explicit treatment focus for two juvenile prostitution programs I contacted during this study.[14]

Although participants in our program often presented an appearance of bravado and toughness, many young women eventually revealed feeling extremely critical about themselves. Many spoke of their pasts with sadness and embarrassment, describing school experiences as difficult and peer relationships as poor.

Many participants said that they had been labeled as "sluts" by schoolmates and parents.

Sexual labeling is strongly linked to the self-concepts of teenage women in trouble. The most important precursor to prostitution for all women consists of sexual experience and conditioning which direct them to define their self-worth in sexual terms.[15]

Each time that a young prostitute has been through the juvenile justice system and in detention, her negative sexual labeling is reinforced. Whatever her crime may be, even if it is shoplifting, her behavior is likely to be associated with her sexuality by juvenile authorities.[16]

Among adolescents, low self-esteem appears to be more characteristic of females than of males. Teenage women are particularly vulnerable to poor self-image during pubertal development and at the onset of dating. Low self-esteem is characteristic of both delinquent and pregnant teens.[17]

Not infrequently, the young women participants in our groups compared themselves to the "home girls," as street youth called teenagers who were not in trouble and who lived at home. These comparisons had a double edge to them: although young prostitutes felt that their street savvy and sophistication placed them above non-prostitutes, underneath that reactive sense of superiority were feelings of being an outcast.

Goal two: improve problem-solving skills. During field research, young women on the streets and in detention came to us with numerous immediate and ongoing problems. These often involved conflicts with family, friends, and others. We observed that these young women often reacted to interpersonal problems aggressively and violently, or, when fulfilling the needs of pimps and customers, passively. Studies confirm that young prostitutes and other delinquents do have deficiencies in problem-solving, assertion, and interpersonal skills.[18]

Goal three: increase women's health knowledge. Young women we met on the streets requested assistance with health problems, especially gynecological problems caused by frequent sex with multiple partners. As mentioned earlier, a consequence of street life is unhealthy living patterns and poor health care. A needs assessment conducted in 1981 by Project S.T.A.R.T. among street clients in Seattle revealed that 16 percent reported a history of sexually transmitted disease (S.T.D.), 58 percent of female clients had never used birth control, and 72 percent had been pregnant.[19]

The high incidence of childbearing among this population may be influenced by an attitude many of them expressed, that if they could take care of themselves, they could care for a child. I could also sense their longing to create the sort of loving family environment they had missed. Most of the young women in the detention sexuality groups I conducted voiced negative opinions about abortion and would rarely admit to having had one. No method of contraception was popular with these young women. Many stated that they did not like to use contraceptives with a boyfriend, because it was unromantic or showed they didn't care. While they did not want to become pregnant by a customer, only a few said they used birth control during business, and that was usually for the prevention of S.T.D.

Goal four: encouraging positive female relationships. Young women living on the streets usually have few positive relationships with other women. Although young prostitutes work together in the same street locations, and some do become friends, there is a constant undercurrent of competition and mistrust.

The longer a young woman remains on the streets, the greater will be her distance from former relationships, and the fewer role models she will have of women who are not part of the street scene. In addition, the pervasiveness of disruption and abuse in the family backgrounds of adolescent prostitutes suggests that relatively few of them had adequate female role models when they were younger. Their mothers may have been physically abused, or themselves abusers. It is important that these young women, like other adolescents, be able to look to adult women as positive role models and to form supportive relationships with adult and adolescent women.

The majority of young prostitutes we interviewed and worked with held stereotypical and restricted views of being a woman. They appeared to prefer a passive and dependent role in their relationships with men, and to expect to be taken care of by a man. Few had plans for a career or lifestyle that would allow them personal and financial autonomy.

Intervention Description:
A Self-esteem Workshop for Young Women

This three-day self-esteem workshop for teenage women has seven components, and each component includes up to six sessions. Although component order is somewhat flexible, individual sessions should be scheduled in the order in which they appear below. This flexible ordering of components and sessions is an advantage when you are trying to schedule volunteer instructors for such sessions as self-defense and dance, as the workshop can then be organized to fit in with volunteer availability. It is a good idea to schedule physically active and inactive sessions alternately, in order to vary the pace of the workshop. Long sedentary "thinking" sessions, especially problem-solving, are best followed by physically active sessions or meal breaks.

Component I. Introduction and Warmup

Time: 30 minutes.
Materials: blackboard or large paper and felt pen.

This session sets the tone for the workshop: relaxed, but focused on important issues; humorous, yet work-oriented; open and sharing, yet respectful of others' right to privacy. Leaders should pay special attention during the group discussions in this session to encouraging the participation of group members while respecting their right to remain silent. These early discussions should begin the process which insures that all participants have a chance to share their feelings and ideas.

Instead of having discipline matters decided by an "authority," the group should develop guidelines. This democratic discipline reinforces the concept that the workshop is not a "treatment" forced on participants, but a participatory experience.

Introductions. Workshop staff members introduce themselves, telling something about their background and what they like to do for fun. This is a time to be personal and humorous, perhaps joking about yourself or your leisure pursuits.

Ask participants to introduce themselves and to say a few words about something that they like to do for fun. Get everyone laughing.

The purpose of the workshop. Explain the purpose of the workshop and the importance of self-esteem. "How we feel about ourselves affects our happiness and performance. How we feel about ourselves is affected by how we think others see us, how we feel about our bodies, our looks, our personality, our abilities, our talents, our future."

Ask participants to list some of the things in their lives (e.g., grades, parents, friends, looks) that affect how they feel about themselves. "These things and people affect our self-esteem, but how *we* view *ourselves* also affects our self-esteem. How we feel about ourselves can influence how our life goes. If we think we have the right to 'make it' in life, that positive feeling can give us the energy to get there."

Workshop schedule. Explain the workshop schedule for the three days. Point out that all sessions relate to self-esteem. For example, "The self-defense class is intended to teach you how to defend yourselves from an attack. When we feel better about our ability to protect ourselves, we feel more confident in general. The problem-solving sessions are also meant to give you more control over your lives. When we know how to handle difficult situations that come up with other people, we feel better about ourselves."

Workshop guidelines. Explain the roles of both self-disclosure and confidentiality (privacy) in the workshop. "Just a moment ago [during the introductions], we shared some information about ourselves. Some of these things may not be very sensitive, but then something one of you just said may be very private. Nothing said in the workshop should ever be talked about outside in a way to identify the person. Leaders will be bound by the same guidelines. You also don't have to say anything you wish to keep private. While it is okay to ask about another's opinion or feelings, it's not a good idea to pressure anyone to talk. We should give everyone a chance to speak, because the more we can open up and share our feelings, the better results we'll be likely to get from the workshop."

Ask participants what they can do to help everyone participate. Also ask what kinds of discipline problems could come up in the workshop and how they could be dealt with. Ask participants to list possible discipline problems and solutions. Write these on the blackboard.

Component II: Group-Building Exercises

SESSION A: PLANNING TOGETHER

Time: 20–30 minutes. (This session should come immediately after *Introductions.*)

Materials: large sheet of paper, felt pen.

Background. The purpose of both group tasks is to encourage positive group process, especially in helping participants to recognize that they have tastes and ideas in common and can work effectively together toward a common plan. By planning some aspect of the workshop, participants can begin to exercise some control over their experience. This first task introduces the process of brainstorming which is later practiced in the problem-solving session.

Group exercise. Explain to participants that they will have fifteen minutes to plan some aspect of the workshop, such as a special activity or one of the meals. Instruct participants to "brainstorm" a number of ideas, then choose among them, and come to a consensus about a menu or an activity. Have one person in the group write down all the initial brainstorming ideas and then the final plan on a large sheet of paper. Notify participants when five minutes remain, so that they can begin the final plan. Wrap up the exercise by having one of the participants explain the plan to the leaders.

SESSION B: FUTURE PLANS

Time: 30 minutes. (This session should be scheduled at the end of the workshop.)

Materials: large paper and felt pen.

Background. To obtain closure to the workshop, this exercise is an opportunity for participants to express their feelings about the workshop as a whole, about other participants, and about staff. Group identification is encouraged and the possibility of ongoing group contact is offered.

Group exercise. Explain to participants that since this is the end of the workshop, it is time to think about what the group might do in the future. Explain that they will have fifteen minutes to discuss what they may wish to plan to do together after the workshop ends (a reunion, more meetings?). The plan should include when, where, frequency of meetings, purpose of meetings, structure of group, name of group, or whatever is necessary to pin down any future get-together. Notify participants when five minutes remain.

Conclude workshop with participants' discussion of their feelings about the workshop experience and its coming to an end.

Component III. Self-Esteem

The self-esteem sessions should be given in order, interspersed with other components.

SESSION A: HOW WE SEE OURSELVES

Time: 30 minutes.

Materials: index cards and pencils.

Background. The purpose of this exercise is to encourage participants to explore their own sense of identity in a playful and nonthreatening way and to begin to share personal aspects of themselves.

If I were a flower. Pass out an index card and a pencil to each participant. Instruct each participant to write down the name of the flower she would be if she were a flower. She is not to choose her favorite flower, but rather a flower she identifies with, that is most like her. Ask each participant to tell the group which flower she chose and a few reasons for her choice; i.e., why that flower is like her.

If I were an animal, if I were a color. Ask each participant to write down on the index card the animal she would be and then the color she would be.

Again ask participants to share their thoughts with the group. Have participants break into two smaller groups, with a leader facilitating each group. Participants discuss the characteristics they associate with the animals and the colors they chose and the reasons for their choices. The leader may also participate in this exercise and explain her choices. If time remains, a general discussion of how people see themselves can conclude this session.

SESSION B: GIVING AND RECEIVING COMPLIMENTS

Time: 20–30 minutes.

Materials: none, or could use index cards for compliment communication.

Background. In this session participants have an opportunity to learn how others see them and to practice social skills in offering and receiving feedback. The exercise also promotes general good feelings between participants, while increasing individual participants' sense of favorable appraisal by others.

Discussion. Discuss the value of compliments and positive feedback. "How do compliments make us feel—as givers and as receivers? People who feel good about themselves are more likely to give sincere compliments." Discuss types of compliments: on appearance, clothes, personality (give example), and actions and behavior (give example).

Accepting a compliment. "Receiving a compliment can be difficult or awkward." Ask a participant to give the leader a compliment. Encourage humor. Leader makes an awkward response to the compliment: "Oh, that's not so great," or, "That's not true." Ask participants to suggest responses that would reflect a more positive self-image.

Giving a compliment. Participants seat themselves in a circle. Each participant then gives a compliment, verbally or in writing, to the person on her right, but no one is to respond to the compliment she receives. Leader may join the circle and participate.

Ask everyone how they felt *receiving* a compliment.

Now each participant gives a compliment to the person on her left. Instruct receivers to respond briefly. "How did it feel to give a compliment? How did it feel to receive a compliment and respond?"

Briefly discuss with participants how it feels in general to get a sincere compliment. "Does it matter what you're complimented about and who gives the compliment?" Ask participants to recall times when someone paid them a compliment and it really felt good.

SESSION C: MY MOTHER, MYSELF

Time: 20–30 minutes
Materials: none.

Background: A purpose of this session is to introduce in a relevant and clear way the concept that women's personalities are strongly influenced by early significant role models, especially mothers or female guardians. Many of the participants (especially those who have run away) may have negative feelings about their mothers; they may also fear that they are destined to repeat aspects of their mothers' lives, such as alcoholism, prostitution, or victimization by battering. This session emphasizes the power we all have to evaluate the role modeling we may have internalized, to find new role models, and to choose our own paths.

An additional purpose of the session is to encourage intimate sharing between participants in a safe environment and to reduce the isolation of young women who have had difficult or abusive family relationships. This session may bring up very strong feelings, and leaders should be alert to the possible need for follow-up sessions with individual participants.

Discussion. Explain social learning simply: "A lot about who we are and how we behave and feel is *learned* from important adults around us as we grow up, especially from our mothers or step/foster mothers. Just as we have learned from important adults and others how to live our lives, we can learn from them how not to live our lives. We can emulate other people of our choice."

Ask participants to mention things they respect about their mothers. In what ways are they like their mothers? Do they like or dislike the behavior they have adopted from their mothers?

Ask each girl to mention something about her mother's personality or behavior that she does not wish to emulate. Why?

Discuss the ways in which our lives today are different from our mothers' or grandmothers'. "Today women have more opportunities to be who they want to be. More women today want to be able to support themselves and have interesting jobs. Women are expecting more equality in their relationships with men, not only sharing the housework, but being treated as an equal in all matters. Women who have been battered or raped are increasingly speaking up."

End the session on the positive note that today women can choose from a greater variety of female role models and ways of living than was possible in the past.

SESSION D: WHAT IS A "REAL WOMAN"?

Time: 30 minutes.

Materials: felt pens, large sheets of paper, and a blackboard.

Background. The purpose of this session is to introduce alternative and expanded definitions of being female. Leaders do not lecture on their beliefs but rather, along with participants, can disclose their own experiences of the social limitations and advantages of being female. Some of the material brought up in the preceding session ("My Mother, Myself") may be utilized by examining messages participants received from their mothers about being female.

This session provides an alternative to the implications of a promise often made by pimps (or boyfriends), "I'll make a *real* woman out of you."

Small group exercise. Introduce the general idea of the exercise: "We are going to look at what it means to be a woman. In your opinion, what are some of the good things in this society about being female, and what are some of the disadvantages?" The leader may offer her own opinion as an example: "I don't like that my husband expects me to do most of the housework even though we both work. He probably feels this way because he was taught that housework is a woman's job."

Have participants break into small groups of about four each. Ask each group to make a list of at least five advantages and five disadvantages of being a woman. Time the session for ten minutes.

Ask a member of each small group to share their list with the whole group. Discuss similarities and differences in the lists and how we might overcome some of the disadvantages of being a woman.

What is a "real woman"? Explain to participants that everyone is strongly influenced by social stereotypes of females and males. These stereotypes lead us to ascribe certain mental, emotional, and behavioral characteristics to females; for example, females are expected to be weak, submissive, gentle, caring, talkative, emotional, bird-brained. Do participants see some of these characteristics as more female than male? Are some or all of these characteristics human rather than female? List on the blackboard words participants suggest to describe a "real woman." Encourage differences of opinion and debate about the list.

End the session by discussing the possibilities for expanding our idea of what it is to be female and how our lives can reflect these broader definitions.

SESSION E: PRIVATE THOUGHTS AND SELF-IMAGE

Time: 15–30 minutes.
Materials: index cards and pencils.

Background. The purpose of this exercise is to train participants to alter self-critical thoughts and increase positive self-evaluations. Research has demonstrated that negative self-appraisals are self-defeating and that self-criticism problems are improved by training which increases the frequency of positive self-statements.[20]

Explanation of self-critical thoughts. "What we say to ourselves (silent thoughts) is a reflection of how we feel about ourselves. Self-confident people usually think positively about themselves. Depressed people and people who feel bad about themselves say more negative things to themselves than do happier and more confident people. If we think we may 'goof up' we are more likely to do so. What we say to ourselves affects our performance and how others view us."

The group leader gives examples of self-critical statements. She verbalizes private thoughts she might have when facing an anxiety-producing situation, such as giving a public talk or making a complaint to her boss. "Oh, my God, I know I'm going to forget my speech," "I must look fat standing up here,"etc.

Looking at our thoughts exercise. Pass out index cards to participants. Ask everyone to write down their first self-evaluating thoughts in reaction to the following three situations read aloud to the group.

Situation one: "A friend comes up to you and says, 'Hey, I

hear there's a job at this real fancy boutique. Why don't you apply for it?'" (Leader may elaborate a bit.) Give participants a moment to write down their thoughts. Ask them to read aloud their immediate thoughts in response to this suggestion.

Situation two: "A counselor (or probation officer) says, 'Why don't you try to go to college? You're smart.'" Ask participants again to write down and then share their private thoughts in response to this suggestion. Indicate which thoughts are positive and which are negative.

Situation three: "A boyfriend says, 'Hey, you look really fine tonight, baby!'" Ask participants what they would say to themselves in this situation.

What to do about negative thoughts. "How would the thoughts we've just heard expressed affect us? Can we change the negative ones?" Give a brief explanation of how to replace negative self-statements with positive ones. "It's a good idea to jot down these kinds of statements for a couple of days—or you can just become aware of them. Then you can start making some honest and positive replacements. For example, let's say I'm about to apply for a job. Instead of thinking, 'I'll never get it,' I could practice saying or thinking, 'I've got just as good a chance as anyone else, and if I really put some thought and care into the application, I might get it.'"

"If we notice our self-statements we can consciously begin to change them." Ask each participant to give an example of a positive self-statement she could make in a real-life situation.

SESSION F: IDEAL SELF-IMAGE

Time: 30–45 minutes.
Materials: none.

Background. The purpose of this guided imagery exercise is to provide participants with a positive vision of their futures—futures that they think could happen.[21] Teenagers like to daydream anyway, and here they can consciously "program" their minds to prepare for the kind of future they choose.

Explanation of exercise. "You've probably heard about programming computers. Did you know that it is also possible to program our minds? That means that you can use the power of your minds to plan your lives. I don't mean that you can become anything in the world you might fantasize, but rather that you can imagine your goals, fix them firmly in your mind, and thereby have some control over where you're heading.

"One way to clarify your goals is to have an idea of what you want to be like—your ideal self. Not someone else, but yourself, with your basic ingredients, as you would like to be and could be. Knowing as much as possible about the self you want to be can help you to choose goals that are right for you and likely to be satisfying."

How we feel about ourselves now. "First let's look at how we feel about ourselves. What do we like about ourselves? Let's see if we can compliment ourselves." Ask that each participant name one thing that she likes about herself. Then ask participants to think of several more things they like about themselves and, if they wish, share these thoughts with the group.

"Now try to think of one thing you don't like about yourself that you can change." Ask each participant to tell one thing about herself that she would like to change.

Guided imagery exercise. "Now we're going to have you try to imagine your ideal self, that is, someone who is really you with all your good qualities. But in addition, you've improved yourself, added some extra good qualities, and perhaps made some changes. You're as you would like to be and could possibly be." Have participants lie down, close their eyes, and deepen their breathing. Spend about a minute or two. Use breath focus to relax participants. "Focus on your breathing. Become very conscious of the air going in and out of your lungs. Feel your breath against the skin inside your nostrils. Deepen your breathing but keep it at a fairly normal rhythm.

"Imagine your ideal self. Imagine youself as you would like to be in, let's say, a year. Picture yourself alone wherever you are living." Pause a minute. "Imagine your environment and picture how you look and feel. Pay attention to what you are doing. Even how you are feeling." Pause a minute. "Now imagine your ideal self walking down the street and meeting someone you know. As your ideal self, how would you act and how would you feel? Go over all of this in your imagination."

Spend about ten minutes on this guided fantasy, and suggest

more experiences, if most participants appear to be concentrating on the exercise. Slowly bring participants out of the guided imagery experience by having them focus again on breathing, and count breaths backwards three, two, one, and then open eyes. Suggest that they will feel relaxed but energetic when they open their eyes.

Ask if any participants would like to tell the group how they felt as their ideal selves.

Suggest that we can use this type of imagery to help us live the kinds of lives we want to live. "When we daydream, we are doing the same sort of thing you've just done. Our daydreams can give us direction for our lives, because unlike the dreams we have when we're asleep, daydreams are under our control. If we become discouraged at times, we can use this exercise to remind ourselves of the goals we want to achieve."

Component IV. Sexuality: Coercion vs. Choice

Time: 2 hours. (This component may be divided into two sessions.)

Materials: blackboard, two rape acquaintance films: "The Party" and "The Gang" (can be purchased through M.T.I. Tele-programs, Inc., 4825 N. Scott Street, Shiller Park, Illinois 60176. Often available through state film libraries and rape counseling services).

Background. The primary purpose of this component is to help participants determine and act upon the rights they have over their own bodies, and to develop positive feelings about their sexuality. Although most teenage women do not admit to gay relationships or feelings, it is important for leaders to mention that homosexuality is the sexual orientation of a number of women and men. Leaders may have to respond to negative stereotypes of gay people expressed by participants.

Role playing of assertive behavior in sexual harassment situations is practiced in conjunction with discussion of two films about acquaintance rape. If you are not familiar with role playing, you can learn its essentials by consulting any one of several excellent guides.[22] You need not be a sexuality expert to lead this session, but some background reading might help you feel more comfortable with explicit or specialized sexuality material.[23]

This component includes material on rape, and is also likely to lead to the subject of incest, areas which may be very sensitive for some participants. Leaders should prepare the group by explaining that they need not talk about their own experiences and that the leader is available after the session, or at other times during the workshop, to talk with participants individually about these issues.

Positive and negative sex. "Sexuality is a powerful thing. Sex can be a very positive as well as very negative experience. It gives us highs sometimes and lows at other times."

Ask participants to suggest examples of sexual experiences that are positive in peoples' lives and those which are negative. When participants mention any type of sexual coercion, such as incest and rape, emphasize that the victim is not to blame, that adults are in a position of power over children, and men are in a position of unequal power with women. Make clear that rape is not an act of sexual passion, but a crime of violence. Elaborate on positive kinds of sexual experiences, those which involve caring relationships, sexual pleasure, and the communication of feelings. Above all, these relationships are mutually desired, and neither party feels forced to have sex.

Ask participants for their views on "one night stands." This question gives participants an opportunity to debate among themselves the advantages of brief sexual encounters and longer term relationships.

Sexual Exploitation. Rape film one: Show rape acquaintance film, "The Party" (20 minutes). (You may follow the discussion guide that comes with the film.) In this film, a young woman meets a young man at a party who eventually forces her to have sex. Between the time of their initial meeting and the rape, she tries unsuccessfully to get out of the situation. The film discussion should include situations in a continuum ranging from sexual harassment to rape. Ask participants to give examples of forms of harassment and abuse in this continuum; i.e., obscene telephone calls. "While there are many situations in which it is impossible for a woman to protect herself from rape, there may also be situations in which you feel uncomfortable (like the young woman in this film), yet you may be afraid to act on your feelings. Sometimes, especially with a boyfriend, you may not feel you have a right to say no. Other times you may know that you do not want sexual contact, but you do not know how to be assertive."

The following role play provides practice in responding assertively to a sexual harassment situation. Ask two participants to volunteer to play the incident before the group.

Role play: A young woman wants advice about what to do about her boss, who is making passes at her. She really wants to keep her job at his restaurant, and she does not want to have sex with him. Recently, he has become more insistent. The young woman asks her friend what she ought to do.

At the conclusion of the role play, ask the group for comments. Leaders should also give feedback.

Rape film two: Show the second rape acquaintance film, "The Gang" (20 minutes). This film is about the rape of one high school student by another. The young woman who is raped appears to have been labelled a "slut" by the males at her school. Discuss the "double standard" in society which allows freedom in sexual behavior for males, while narrowly defining the sexual behavior allowed "good girls." Discuss the connection between a young woman's sexual reputation and her feelings about herself. During group discussion of the film, encourage participants to suggest ways in which the young woman in the film might have protected herself through assertive behavior. Emphasize that she is in no way to "blame" for the rape. There is never an "excuse" for rape; the rapist is fully responsible for his act. Nevertheless, in some situations, paying attention to one's feelings and acting assertively may reduce the risks of being raped.

The following role play allows participants to practice responding assertively to the circumstance of being labelled a "slut." Ask participants to pair up and role play the situation with one another, allowing five minutes for this part of the exercise.

Role play: A young woman tells her friend about the problem she is having in a new school she's attending, where she is working on her G.E.D. She has discovered that a young man, also a student in the school, is telling everyone that she's a whore. This deeply troubles the young woman, but she doesn't know what to do about it. She asks her friend for advice.

Participants return to the group and share their ideas of possible solutions.

Positive aspects of female sexuality. "From the discussions we've just had, it might seem that sex is always a problem, but this isn't true. Early on in this session we mentioned that sex can be a very positive experience, and now we're going to talk about how this is so."

Sexual response cycle: Describe the four stages of sexual response (excitement, plateau, orgasm, and resolution) and draw a graph on the blackboard. Describe the specific physical signs of arousal and orgasm (vaso-congestion and muscular tension).[24]

Orgasm: "What is an orgasm? What does it feel like? How do you know if you have one? Do you need one?" (Many teenage women have not experienced an orgasm, and others may be embarrassed to discuss their experiences.) The leader may choose to give a general description of female arousal and orgasm, emphasizing that individual women experience these sensations differently.

Masturbation: Ask the group what they think of masturbation. Dispell any false notions about its being harmful. Mention that masturbation is a normal practice of both females and males. Most teenagers deny masturbating and feel that it is a bad thing for others to do. You might mention that according to a study on teenage sexuality, the majority of teenagers said they masturbated.[25]

Sex for communication and intimacy: Discuss the ways in which sex can help us feel closer to someone we care for. Reciprocal sexual intimacy is one of many avenues for communication of our feelings of tenderness and affection. "When we love someone romantically, we want to demonstrate our love in many ways. One way is through touching. There is a natural physical attraction, a 'chemistry' that we experience with someone we love. Sometimes we want to squeeze our lover's hand; sometimes we want to hug or kiss; sometimes we want to have sex. In all these ways we share our loving feelings with a partner."

Sex by choice: Discuss the various ways women may recognize their desire to make love. "Women can get turned on just by seeing or thinking about an attractive person. We may become aroused by touching or being touched by our partners. Sometimes we begin to feel the physical changes we discussed earlier (increased breathing, special sensations in the genital area, etc.). Sometimes we may just feel the need for closeness and hugging and not want to have sex. Then we need to feel free to communicate these feelings to our partner, and not have sex just because we think it is expected of us."

Component V. Problem Solving and Social Skills

The purpose of both sessions is to train participants to solve interpersonal problems in ways which are effective in conventional society. Young women who have lived on the streets or in a correctional institution have learned other ways, usually either passive or hostile, of dealing with conflict. Examples of social problem situations utilized here are drawn from events likely to arise in participants' lives. Solutions reinforced are those which are assertive and appropriate in conventional society. The problem-solving training method used here is adapted from D'Zurilla and Goldfried.[26]

Because problem-solving training is complex, it is especially important that the sessions be lively and interesting. Examples chosen to illustrate the problem-solving steps can be humorous. Lectures should be brief, and leaders should encourage a maximum of participation.

SESSION A

Time: 1–1½ hours.
Materials: blackboard or large sheets of paper and felt pen; chart of four problem-solving steps.

Introduction. Begin by stating that it is normal to have problems; obviously, we all do. The leader should give a humorous example of a personal problem. A co-leader may offer a humorous solution and then a serious one.

Discuss differences between straight world and street world problem solving. "Today we'll be talking about how to solve problems in the straight world rather than in the street world. Can any of you give an example of the differences between straight world and street world solutions?"

Big and little problems. Discuss the benefits of effective problem solving. "If we let a lot of little problems accumulate, then we find ourselves with a problem that might be too big to tackle. So it's important to work on little problems before they grow. For example, imagine that you're starting to get angry with your boy-friend. He rarely shows up when he says he will. You could just let this go on for a long time, maybe because you're hoping he'll change or maybe because you're uncomfortable talking to him about this. Instead, imagine that after the first time he fails to meet you and doesn't apologize, you ask him what caused the problem. You explain to him that it is important to be able to count on each other."

Ask participants for other examples of little problems that can grow into big ones.

Overview of four problem-solving steps. Provide a brief explanation of the four basic problem-solving steps, using a chart which lists the steps. Keep this chart visible during both problem-solving sessions, so that participants can refer back to it. Read aloud the short description of each step outlined below. (During the remainder of the two sessions, each step will be explored in detail.)

1. Describe the problem.

Explain what the problem is, especially by specifying; i.e., giving specific examples of how, when, and with whom the problem has occurred.

2. Brainstorm.

Think up as many ideas for solutions as possible. Be creative, and don't judge your ideas yet.

3. Evaluate.

Evaluate your ideas and state reasons why it's a good or bad idea. Put a + or − after each idea, depending on whether you think it's a good idea or an ineffective one.

4. Choose a solution and develop a plan.

Choose the best solution available, either one of those you've listed or a combination of a couple of ideas. Now decide on a plan of action: what, when, where, how. Figure out possible obstacles to the plan and prepare for them if you can.

Step 1. Describe the problem.

Demonstration. Explain that it is necessary to specify aspects of a general problem to understand it more fully and to develop an effective solution. Explain that to "specify" means to break down a general problem ("I hate school") into smaller parts ("I failed math; my teacher blames me for disturbances; I feel left out by other kids"). In describing a problem it is as important to get at facts ("I failed math") as at feelings ("I feel left out").

On the blackboard, make a list of both generally stated and specified problems. Examples may be suggested by the leader or by participants.

Examples (do not add information in parentheses):

I hate school. (General.)

My probation officer hates me. (General.)

My boyfriend treats me bad. (General.)

Two girls in the unit call me "creep" whenever they talk to me. (Specific.)

Every time my mother comes to visit she tells me I cause all the problems and then I get mad at her and we start screaming. (Specific.)

Ask participants which problems are general and which are specific. Help them to break down general descriptions of problems into more specific aspects; for example: "What specific things do you hate at school?"

Practice exercise. Ask participants to pair off. One member of the pair describes an interpersonal problem she now has or has had in the past. The other participant helps her to describe the problem fully and break it down into its elements. Allow about five minutes for this step. Leaders should check on pairs and provide help, if needed.

Assemble the whole group. Each pair may describe the problem they are working on, if they wish to do so.

Step 2. Brainstorming.

Explain that the technique of brainstorming is intended to produce as many ideas as possible, without prejudging them. Demonstrate brainstorming by describing an interpersonal problem and asking all participant to suggest ideas for solving the problem. The leader should describe an interpersonal problem that she is facing or has faced in her own life. She should briefly specify the various aspects of the problem. Participants will be more interested in suggesting ideas if they feel that the problem is a "serious" one and that they can help the leader. Make a blackboard list of their suggested solutions.

Practice exercise. Ask participants to pair off with the partners they had in the previous exercise and to brainstorm at least three or four ideas for solving the problem they are working on. Allow about ten minutes for this process. Leaders circulate and coach pairs if needed.

Assemble the whole group and ask participants to share their ideas. Encourage feedback from the group.

Step 3. Evaluate.

Demonstration. Explain evaluation criteria: Will it be effective? Can it be done? Do I have the skills to do it? What are the consequences? Will it get me in trouble? Will it get the other person mad at me so that things are worse later? Also discuss the ethical implications of the ideas. Will this hurt someone? What are my values?

Return to the demonstration example from II (i.e., leader's problem) and ask participants to evaluate the ideas generated earlier, putting a + or − after each one.

Practice exercise. Ask participants to return to their pairs and evaluate their previously generated ideas. They are to give reasons for assigning a + or − to each idea. Allow about ten minutes, and therapists coach as needed.

Assemble the whole group and take a stretch break.

Step 4. Choose a solution and develop a plan.

Demonstration. Review the elements of choosing a solution and making a plan. "Choose the idea you think best solves the problem or perhaps combine two or more ideas. Now make an action plan including who, when, what, and where."

Return to the problem example demonstrated in steps 2 and 3 and demonstrate the processes of choosing a solution and making a plan by enlisting suggestions from participants.

Practice exercise. Ask participants to reform into the same pairs for about ten minutes, to choose a solution and develop a plan.

Again, leaders should assist as necessary.

Have everyone rejoin the group and share their final solutions and plans of action. Encourage feedback from the group.

This last step may be saved for the next session if time runs out or if participants are fatigued. In order that participants remain interested throughout the problem-solving training, leaders should monitor their level of enthusiasm and adjust the pacing and material accordingly.

Session B

Time: 1–1½ hours.

Materials: blackboard or large paper and felt pen, and problem-solving steps chart.

Review. Review all the problem-solving steps briefly. Give participants positive feedback on the work they did in Session A. If the fourth step, "choose a solution," was not completed in the first session (A), do so.

Four-step practice. Ask participants to form into the same pairs as in Session A. Now participants exchange roles; the participant who did not work on her problem in the first session now chooses a problem to be worked on. Tell participants they have fifteen minutes to go through all four problem-solving steps and arrive at a solution and a plan of action. Leaders should assist any pairs who ask for help. Leaders may help with the problem-solving process, but should not suggest ideas.

Assemble the whole group and ask participants to report on how the exercise went. "Did the four steps make it easier to solve the problem? Do you think you might use this method on your own?" Ask whether any of the participants would like to state briefly the problem and the solution plan of her pair.

Social skill role play. Explain that practicing the interpersonal part of your plan with a friend can be very useful. "Practice can help you feel more confident and relaxed. It can also help you polish what you're going to say and how you might respond. By practicing what you are going to say [as part of the solution plan] and having your friend play the other person, you get a chance to experiment and receive feedback."

Ask one of the pairs to volunteer to role play an interpersonal aspect of their solution plan before the whole group. Staff and participants should give supportive feedback.

Relaxation and private rehearsal. Ask participants to lie down in a comfortable position.

Explain that we can also practice problem-solving in our imaginations. "In a minute I am going to help you to relax and get into a calm headspace so that you can begin to imagine successfully doing the part of your plan that involves another person." Instruct participants to use the problem they have just worked on, or another one.

Relaxation: Provide suggestions for using the breath to induce relaxation (2–3 minutes). "Focus your attention on your breathing. Feel your breath moving in and out of your lungs. Feel the air move against the inside of your nostrils." Suggest deepening the breath and clearing the mind with each exhalation.

Guided imagery: Begin the guided imagery exercise: "Keep your eyes closed and imagine that you are successfully dealing with your problem. Notice who you are interacting with. Notice what you feel. You are feeling confident about what you are doing." (Allow a minute or two to pass.) "In a moment finish your interaction and give yourself a pat on the back. Now focus again on your breathing." (Pause a moment.) Bring yourself back to this room by imagining what it looks like. Slowly open your eyes."

Ask for feedback from participants about their experiences during the relaxation and guided imagery exercises.

Component VI. Women's Health

Time: 1–1½ hours.

Materials: Women's Health Test; samples of birth control devices; anatomy and physiology charts; handouts on contraceptive methods, STD, and sources of care.

Background. This component should be led by a female health professional who specializes in women's health care, such as a nurse practitioner. Lectures should be brief, and the content that is emphasized in the session should be guided by participants' questions.

Introduction. Have the instructor introduce herself and tell about her work in women's health care, citing specific examples of problems teenagers bring to her.

Test and discussion. Give participants a brief multiple-choice test which covers the topics included in this session. (A test is provided at the end of this article; the health instructor may wish to substitute her own test.) Explain that participants are not expected to know the correct answers to all questions; in cases of doubt they should record their best guesses. All questions on the test will be addressed in this session. Participants should keep their completed tests for their private reference as the session proceeds.

Provide the correct answers to questions and use the test structure to initiate discussion about female reproductive anatomy and physiology, the most common sexually transmitted infections in men and women, fertile period, abortion and contraception (types, reliability, and safety.) Pass around actual birth control devices. Although all the above topics should be mentioned, the discussion should be guided by what interests participants most.

Sexually transmitted disease slides. Show slides illustrating some of the symptoms of common S.T.D.'s. S.T.D. slides can usually be found through public S.T.D. clinics and medical schools. Discuss prevention and treatment.

Sources of health care. Discuss community resources for health care, especially for contraception, S.T.D., and abortion. Explain usual procedures for making appointments at public clinics.

Component VII. Body Image and Awareness

The following sessions provide a necessary change of pace from the physically inactive, cognitive-behavioral components. They should be interspersed with sessions in the preceding componnents and may be scheduled in any order, although "Personal Appearance" should be scheduled at a time when participants might best be able to "show off" their new appearances.

The instructors for these sessions should be trained persons who are willing to volunteer their services. In most large communities there are fashion and beauty consultants who have presented programs for women's groups and who may be called upon to develop a session especially for this workshop.

The main purpose of the sessions is to expand participants' experiences of feeling good about their bodies. Beauty is defined to include good grooming, physical fitness, and physical self-confidence. Sexual allure is de-emphasized.

Throughout the workshop, group leaders act as role models. The volunteer staff in this component provide additional, alternative role models.

These sessions should be developed by the instructors leading them.

SESSION A: PERSONAL APPEARANCE

Time: 3 hours.

Materials: Polaroid camera and film, hair styling and make-up supplies, material swatches in a variety of colors.

Background. This session is very popular with teenage women. It can be scheduled late in the workshop to maintain enthusiasm, as it is something participants look forward to. Participants are advised on how to choose a wardrobe, apply make-up, and style their hair attractively and appropriately for employment or school. (Young women who have lived on the streets or in institutions often lose jobs because of inappropriate dress and make-up.)

The session should be developed and led by a team of three beauticians. While one instructor lectures, the other two style participants' hair and apply their make-up. In this way, every participant may have a "make-over" if she wishes, while at the same time all participants can listen to lectures and participate in the discussions.

It is important that the beauticians be skilled in the beauty care of black women and that pictures used as examples include minority as well as white women.

The session outlined below provides a guide for organizing the material; the guide can be made available to the volunteer staff.

Introduction. Beautician instructors introduce themselves and talk a little about their work with teenage clients. Below is an example of an opening talk.

"You're only as pretty as you feel, because the aura of personal beauty a woman projects is really an indefinable property that each of us measures against our own preferences and prejudices. And, even if some great omnipotent judge could rank each of us according to sheer physical beauty, our evaluations of each other are always influenced by the power of each individual's degree of self-awareness and self-assuredness. All too often, women will complain that they're not pretty because this feature or that feature is all wrong. Ridiculous! The first step in becoming more beautiful is to *feel* more beautiful—to have pride in what's right about your appearance, rather than yield to what's wrong. Look in the mirror. Surely you see as many assets as liabilities, whether you're plump, thin, light, dark, disabled, tall, or short. Because of its transience, all beauty is an illusion. A young girl may relinquish her physical beauty to time, while another woman will increase in attractiveness with each passing year. It's this characteristic of constant change that makes self-assessment of beauty and self-appreciation so vital. The cultural heritage of Western societies is one that epitomizes the oval or egg as the perfect shaped face; and yet, how many exciting, glamorous women have you seen who have anything but the classic shape? What is their secret? Most certainly, the energy radiating from their secure self-confidence in their own capabilities plays a large part, as well as the knowledge that they've rendered their physical imperfections less visible through the careful selection of hairstyle, make-up and clothing. Why should you not do as well?"

Emphasize throughout the session that while feeling good about one's appearance is an important part of self-esteem, trying to be sexy or pretty primarily to impress others is never satisfying.

Photo. Take a Polaroid "before" photo of each participant.

Color and style analysis. To introduce individual analysis of color and fashion type, hand out a personal inventory chart which analyzes posture, face shape, physique, hair, eyes, and so on. Hold swatches of colored fabric in front of each participant and ask the rest of the group to indicate which colors look best on her.

Hair styling. Begin individual hair cutting and blow drying while individual color and style analyses continue.

Make-up. When all participants who have volunteered to have their hair cut and styled are finished, the individual make-up sessions begin.

Photo. Take a Polaroid "after" photo of each participant. All participants may then view each other's pictures.

Session B: Self-Defense

Time: 1–1½ hours.
Materials: none. Session should take place in a gym or a large room.

Background. The self-defense session should be developed by a female self-defense instructor. The session should emphasize a woman's rights over her own body and the contribution that physical skills can make to the defense of those rights. Discussion of assault may flow from the instructor's descriptions of incidents known to her or from experiences of participants or those of their friends.

As this material is potentially sensitive, it is important that no participant be asked to talk if she wishes to be silent and merely listen. Leaders sitting in on the session should be alert to signs that some participants might welcome individual counseling about past sexual assault; this can be offered privately to such participants without attracting the notice of other members of the group.

Introduction. The self-defense instructor introduces herself and tells about her training and teaching experiences, especially with teenage women.

Discussion. Discuss dangerous situations in which it would be advisable to use self-defense techniques. Invite participants to tell of times when they have been threatened by force or actually physically injured. Be careful to make this a general invitation which allows participants to volunteer information or to refrain from doing so. A number of participants may not wish to talk about their experiences. Mention that learning self-defense techniques helps you feel more secure even if you never have to use them. "Have you ever been out at night when you were constantly afraid that someone would attack you, so that you couldn't relax and enjoy yourself?"

Warmup and strength-building exercises. Show participants how to do warmup and stretching exercises. Explain the importance of warming up for exercise. Demonstrate strength-building exercises.

Self-defense techniques. Instructor demonstrates self-defense techniques. Participants pair off and practice techniques.

Closing discussion. Ask for feedback from participants. Do they feel that any of these techniques could be useful? Under what circumstances and conditions?

SESSION C: DANCE

Time: 1 hour.
Materials: none. Session should be held in a gym or a large open space.

This session should be led by a professional dance teacher who has designed her own class. Emphasis should be on integrating body awareness and self-image with general self-esteem. The instructor should make exercises and routines simple and clear so that every participant can successfully execute them. Choose music that is lively and current, preferably rock-and-roll or jazz.

SESSION D: YOGA

Time: 1 hour.
Materials: none. Session should be held in a fairly large room which is carpeted or furnished with mats for participants.

This session should be led by a professional yoga instructor who has designed her own class. As with the dance class, ask the instructor to teach simple postures so that every participant can execute them easily. Ask the instructor to give a brief explanation of the purpose (not the history) of yoga.

Intervention Evaluation

Three counseling groups of five to eight participants were evaluated, using four assessment measures[27] given pre- and post-intervention, as well as a participant evaluation form and continuous observations noted in a treatment log. A comparison of pre- and posttests showed statistically significant improvement in self-esteem, problem-solving skills, and women's health knowledge.[28] There were no significant differences in score changes between the groups conducted in detention and the group conducted in a private setting.

On a scale of one (very useful) to five (not useful at all), participants gave a high mean usefulness rating of 1.7 for the workshop as a whole. Participants rated the sexuality component as most useful while a decided majority responded that they enjoyed the personal appearance session the most. The problem-solving component elicited relatively low interest and was mentioned by several participants as among the least enjoyable sessions.

Some participants appeared to benefit from the workshop more than others. The most outstanding factor that appeared to affect a young woman's response was what might be termed a "critical incident" in her life prior to group participation. Participants who had recently experienced a dangerous or frightening event such as rape, assault, or arrest, or whose street friend had been hurt or killed seemed to be highly motivated to change their lives and leave the streets. Participants who discussed such an experience during the group were markedly cooperative and positive in the sessions, and stated that they wanted to leave prostitution.

An additional factor which might affect a participant's responsiveness to the intervention is the length of time she has been on the streets and the degree of contact she has maintained with conventional society. Should a critical incident occur which motivates a young prostitute to change her life, actualizing this urge may be too difficult if she has broken her ties with conventional society.

Some young women, especially those who assisted with the field work and the ensuing workshop sessions, formed especially close ties with me and maintained contact after the conclusion of the workshop. Among these participants, at least two report that they have ceased street life and prostitution activities. The use of peer assistants may enhance the impact of the workshop on participants and may benefit the helpers themselves. Former participants, or young women who would qualify as participants and who show a high degree of interest in the intervention, can be selected as workshop assistants. In order to increase the cultural sensitivity and relevancy of the workshop, peer assistants may be involved in formulating and dramatizing interpersonal problem-solving vignettes and role plays. The use of peer assistants may provide group leaders with a source of feedback about the appropriateness of different parts of the intervention and the degree to which group leaders and participants are communicating.

Considerations for Group Leaders

The counseling intervention will be most effective if group leaders are experienced in working with delinquent and runaway girls and are familiar with street language and mores. If the intervention is to be held in a correctional facility, the leader will be confronted with the necessary but difficult task of relating effectively both to clients and correction staff.

It is important that leaders and other staff neither pity nor condemn participants; rather, they should be sensitive to how young street women view their own situations. Attention should be paid to including minority women among group leaders and staff to increase the relevancy of role models for minority participants.

A strong, directive style is effective with this population. As in any classroom situation with adolescents, discipline problems may arise. They can be minimized by leaders' firm and consistent handling of them, which complements the democratic participant-elicited guidelines described earlier.

Conclusion

While an intervention, such as the one developed here, may at least temporarily improve a young woman's self-concept, it cannot change the way she is viewed by society. Programs focused on young prostitutes themselves will not affect the double standard which defines women by their sexuality, nor will such programs affect the practice of juvenile prostitution, as long as there is a market for the sale of young women's sexual services. While it is only humane to act now, with whatever means we have, to reduce the pain and improve the lives of young women engaged in or at risk of prostitution, we must begin to look toward effecting essential change that alters the social conditions upon which juvenile prostitution is based.

Women's Health Test*

1. Women are most likely to get pregnant
   a. during their period
   b. in the week before their period
   c. one week after their period
   d. two weeks before their period
   e. two weeks after their period

---

*Developed by Sharon Baker, R.N., M.P.H., Adult Health Clinic, Harborview Medical Center, Seattle, Washington.

2. You can't get pregnant if a man "pulls out"
   before he comes.
   ☐ True
   ☐ False

3. If you are spotting when you are taking the pill it means your
   pills aren't strong enough and you might get pregnant.
   ☐ True
   ☐ False

4. If you are under eighteen you need your parents' consent to
   get birth control or an abortion.
   ☐ True
   ☐ False

5. Welfare pays for abortions.
   ☐ True
   ☐ False

6. For women who smoke and take birth control pills the risk of
   heart disease is
   a. the same as for women who don't smoke
   b. twice as high
   c. ten times as high

7. Which methods of birth control help protect you from V.D.?
   a. pills
   b. I.U.D.
   c. foam
   d. condoms
   e. diaphragm

8. Symptoms of V.D. in a man could include
   a. a drip from the penis
   b. burning when peeing
   c. sores on the penis
   d. rash on his body
   e. itching between his fingers
   f. sore balls
   g. upset stomach
   h. sore throat
   i. diarrhea
   j. aching joints (knees, etc.)

9. Symptoms of V.D. in a woman could include
   a. low belly pain
   b. sore throat
   c. diarrhea
   d. sores or rash on her body
   e. aching joints
   f. vaginal discharge
   g. vaginal smell
   h. sores on her perineum (pussy)
   i. itching perineum
   j. burning when peeing

10. If a man got a shot for gonorrhea (clap) yesterday it is safe to have sex with him today.
    ☐ True
    ☐ False

11. You can pick up V.D. from a dirty bathroom.
    ☐ True
    ☐ Fålse

12. You can pick up V.D. using a friend's douche set or towel.
    ☐ True
    ☐ False

13. Women who are lovers can give each other V.D.
    ☐ True
    ☐ False

14. If you have V.D. when you are pregnant it can hurt the baby.
    ☐ True
    ☐ False
    ☐ Sometimes

15. If you check carefully you can always tell if a man has V.D.
    ☐ True
    ☐ False

NOTES

1. According to the Federal Bureau of Investigation, female juvenile prostitution increased 183.3 percent between 1969 and 1978. F.B.I., *Uniform Crime Reports* (Washington, D.C.: U.S. Department of Justice, 1979). These figures reflect only arrests. I met many young women in detention and on the streets who had prostitution experience, but who had never been arrested for soliciting.

2. The Shelter, Seattle, Washington.

3. The meetings were scheduled in the early evenings, before the young women began their work on the streets.

4. The young prostitutes usually worked independently during breaks between pimps; we were in contact with many of them during these intervals.

5. "Juvenile Prostitution in Minnesota" (1978) is distributed by the Center for Youth Development and Research, 48 McNeal Hall, University of Minnesota, St. Paul, Minn. 55108.

6. Debra Boyer and Jennifer James, "Easy Money," in *Justice for Young Women: Close-up on Critical Issues,* edited by Sue Davidson (Tucson, Ariz.: New Directions for Young Women, 1982), pp. 73–97; Diana Gray, "Turning Out: A Study of Teenage Prostitution," *Urban Life and Culture* 1 (1973), pp. 401–425.

7. "Juvenile Prostitution," pp. 22–23.

8. Mavis Tsai, Shirley Feldman-Summers and M. Edgar, "Childhood Molestation: Variables Related to Differential Impacts on Psychosexual Functioning in Adult Women," *Journal of Abnormal Psychology* 8, 4 (1981), pp. 407–417.

9. The U.S. General Accounting Office reported in 1982 that there were four residential shelters in the United States. "Sexual Exploitation of Children: A Problem of Unknown Magnitude," Publication H.R.D.-82-64.

10. From a feminist perspective, there is, of course, no logic in abhorring child prostitution while condoning the same exploitation of adult women.

11. For a thorough critique of traditional criminology as applied to prostitutes and other female offenders, see Carol Smart, *Women, Crime, and Criminology* (London: Routledge, Kegan Paul, 1976), or Eileen

Leonard, *Women, Crime, and Society: A Critique of Theoretical Criminology* (New York: Longman, 1982).

12.   See, for example, Gisela Konopka, *The Adolescent Girl in Conflict* (Englewood Cliffs, N.J.: Prentice Hall, 1966).

13.   Dennis Romig, *Justice for Our Children: An Examination of Juvenile Delinquent Rehabilitation Programs* (Lexington, Mass: Lexington Books, 1978), p. 21.

14.   Project S.T.A.R.T., The Shelter, Seattle, and the NewBridge, Minneapolis.

15.   Boyer and James, p. 94.

16.   Meda Chesney-Lind, "Judicial Enforcement of the Female Sex Role: The Family Court and the Female Delinquent," *Issues in Criminology* 8, 2 (1973), pp. 51–70; Leslie S. Smith, "Sexist Assumptions and Female Delinquency," in *Women, Sexuality, and Social Control*, pp. 80–85.

17.   Roberta Simmons, Dale Blythe, Edward Van Cleave, D. Mitsch Bush, "Entry into Early Adolescence: The Impact of School Structure, Puberty, and Early Dating on Self-Esteem," *American Sociological Review* 44 (December 1979), pp. 948–967; W. H. Fitts and W. T. Hammer, *The Self-Concept and Delinquency* (Nashville, Tenn.: Counselor Recordings and Tests, 1965).

18.   V. Little and P. Kendall, "Cognitive Behavioral Interventions with Delinquents," in *Cognitive Behavioral Interventions: Theory, Research, and Procedures*, edited by P. Kendall and S. Hollon (San Francisco: Academic Press, 1979); Michael Mahoney, "Cognitive Issues in the Treatment of Delinquency," in *Progress in Behavior Therapy with Delinquents*, edited by J. S. Stumphauser (Springfield, Ill.: Charles C. Thomas, 1979).

19.   The study was prepared by The Shelter, 1545 Twelfth Ave. S., Seattle, Wash., 98144.

20.   Sharon Berlin, "Cognitive-behavioral Intervention for Problems of Self-criticism among Women," *Social Work Research and Abstracts* 16 (1980), pp. 19–28.

21.   See Dorothy Suskind, "The Idealized Self-Image (I.S.I.): A New Technique in Confidence Training," *Behavior Therapy* 1 (1971), pp. 538–541.

22.   Ginny NiCarthy, *Assertion Skills for Young Women: A Manual* (Tucson, Ariz.: New Directions for Young Women, 1981); Barbara Gates, Susan Klaw, Adria Steinberg, *Changing Learning/Changing Lives: A High School Women's Studies Curriculum from The Group School* (Old Westbury, N.Y.: The Feminist Press, 1979).

23.   Boston Women's Health Collective, *Our Bodies, Ourselves* (New York: Simon and Schuster, 1977); Lonie Barbach, *For Yourself: The Fulfillment of Female Sexuality* (Garden City, N.Y.: Doubleday & Co., 1975).

24.   See William Masters and Virginia Johnson, *Human Sexual Response* (Boston: Little Brown & Co., 1966), p. 5.

25.   Aaron Hass, *Teenage Sexuality* (Los Angeles: Pinnacle Books, 1979), pp. 98–101.

26.   T. D'Zurilla and M. Goldfried, "Problem Solving Behavior Modification," *Journal of Abnormal Psychology* 78 (1971), pp. 107–126.

27.   The measures included the Index of Self-esteem, developed by Walter Hudson, *The Clinical Measurement Package: A Field Practice* (Homewood, Ill.: The Dorsey Press, 1982); a video self-esteem test and a video problem-solving test developed for this evaluation, and a women's health test, also developed for this program.

28.   Index of Self-esteem scores increased from pre- to post-test a mean of 4.9 points ($t = 3.00$, $N = 18$, $p < .01$).
Both video self-esteem scores improved, but the changes were not statistically significant. Both video problem-solving test scores improved: the total number of problem-solving ideas increased an average of 4.5 ideas ($t = 3.28$, $N = 18$, $p < .001$), and the number of effective ideas increased a mean of 4.9 ($t = 4.34$, $N = 18$, $p < .001$). The women's health test scores increased a mean of 3.9 points ($t = 12.32$, $N = 15$, $p < .001$).

More Open Doors: Support for Lesbian and Gay Adolescents

Sue Saperstein

Young gays live with families. We live with families who do not know we are gay. We live with families who know because they "discovered" through some incident or because we've told them. . . . We live with families who beat us up for being gay; who will not allow "queer" friends to come over the house, call on the phone, or go out with their daughters. These are families who will listen in on our phone conversations . . . interrogate callers . . . open and throw away mail, go through drawers, taking zealous measures to root this "evil" out of our lives. We also live with families who coerce us into seeing psychiatrists, who threaten and do hospitalize us and incarcerate us—"If we don't straighten up." Many of us live with families who totally ignore our gayness, thinking "it's just a phase." Nothing like wholesale invalidation. Young gays also don't live with families, for all of the above reasons.[1]

—Thoughts of a young lesbian

Social service professionals who work with adolescents and their families have long overlooked sexual identity as one of the covert problems in a troubled family. Family recognition and acceptance are central to an adolescent's healthy maturation process, and are directly related to the development of a positive self-image.

In an effort to provide a framework for better serving lesbian and gay youth, this article will focus on family dynamics facing lesbian and gay youth, illustrate the need for a family system during •

This article has been expanded and updated since its first printing, under the title, "Lesbian and Gay Adolescents: The Need for Family Support," in *Catalyst* no. 12, copyright ©1981. Used by permission of *Catalyst*.

the critical adolescent stage of development, and discuss one model for providing gay-sensitive support services within a community, with a specific focus on gay-sensitive foster homes.

The Problem: Lack of Family Support

Confronting a child's gayness can create emotional problems, tension, and hostile reactions in even the most open and supportive families. While some parents may adjust to the discovery of their child's homosexuality and offer support and guidance, for many families a child's lesbian or gay sexual identity results in family breakdown and tragedy.

One gay youth described his perceptions of the problems many parents experience:

> It cannot be denied that gayness is still considered abnormal (or worse) by many people, and parents are often prone to misinterpret an honest admission of sexual identity for an accusation of failure on their part. Parents feel extremely threatened by the suggestion of failure, which worsens their feeling of alienation that results from discovering an unknown aspect of a son or daughter they thought they knew well. Many parents avoid the problem of acceptance by ignoring the subject entirely, refusing to admit what is obvious. Some parents reject their child completely, which can be as traumatic to the parent as to the child—although of course, the parent doesn't suffer the terrible things that young people, suddenly on their own, experience.[2]

Contributing to a parent's denial of her or his child's gayness and personal sense of failure is the traditional belief that heterosexuality is healthy and homosexuality is "sick," and the accompanying expectations. Personal biases, and negative judgments regarding *all* adolescent sexuality and activity, make "coming out" to such parents a painful experience for most youth. The following cases illustrate this point:

> Mr. and Mrs. P., from Nevada, came to San Francisco to pick up their sixteen year old son, Jim, at Juvenile Hall. Jim was charged with solicitation. He was released to his parents, referred to the probation depart-

ment in his county of residence, and he and his family were referred to a family therapist. The P.'s left the court together and drove downtown, where Jim's father gave him $50 and told him not to return home.

Lindsay was brought by her athletic coach to see a counselor at a mental health clinic after the coach had noticed bruises on her when she was changing into gym shorts. Although Lindsay had responded defensively to the teacher's initial inquiry, with the teacher's warm and concerned encouragement, Lindsay explained tearfully that she had told her mother that she was a lesbian. Now she is forbidden to go out, and when she tries to leave, her mother beats her and calls her a "sick slut."

Lee, a fourteen year old Asian lesbian, must strip off her clothes when she comes home from school. Her clothes are all marked with red thread to keep them separate from her family's laundry. She must shower before she is allowed to join the family because she is "dirty."

"What did I do wrong?" is the self-blaming and homophobic* reaction many parents have to their child's emerging sexual identity. Parents fear being blamed by people in their community. Lack of access to positive information and resources for parents and youths contributes to the lack of understanding of the problems. Further complicating the family dynamic of negativity and ignorance is the fact that many lesbian and gay youth experience their sexual feelings with a mixture of excitement, pain and confusion, profound loneliness, alienation, and self-rejection. Perceiving their child's pain, parents often become even less accepting or supportive of a gay identity. They do not understand that they and their children share the same internalized homophobia. Their solution will often be that their child should be helped to change and become "normal," further intensifying and reinforcing the rejection and negation of their child's feelings. As the misunderstanding be-

---

*Homophobia: extreme fear or suspicion of lesbians and gay males.

tween parent and child grows, tensions increase, and there is further withdrawal from one another.

Consequences of Family Breakdown

As a result of family breakdown, it is not surprising that lesbian and gay youth have been found to comprise a significant percentage of "beyond parental control" and runaway youth populations. These youth are often "throwaways" because their families have physically and psychologically rejected them, and do not want them to return home.

Many youth leave their homes seeking refuge in large cities. These young people, some as young as twelve years old, are not prepared for independence, and lack the skills necessary to survive and support themselves. Fortunately, some connect with a network of young lesbians and gays who join together to find homes and jobs, and who provide emotional support for one another. The drive appears to be towards creating new familial systems, with lesbian and gay peers or older lesbians and gays fulfilling parental roles. Other youth seek independence and emancipation. Some are victims of their umet needs, abusing drugs and alcohol. Still others resort to suicide as a result of their desperate loneliness.

Statistics compiled by Huckleberry House, a crisis shelter for runaway youth, indicate that in large cities such as San Francisco, there are 500 to 1,000 of these young people on the streets each day.[3] These numbers represent a cross-section of the entire population. The youths come from cities and suburbs, and from working-class and upper-class backgrounds; they are white and Third World.[4] It is important to note that the many uncounted lesbian and gay adolescents who remain at home, invisible and isolated, are not reflected in these statistics.

Undoubtedly, a large percentage of those missing in the statistical count are young lesbians. Several factors contribute to the invisibility of lesbian adolescents. Although the young lesbian may feel different and behave differently than her female peers, she may escape being labelled lesbian or gay during adolescence. Because of the sexual socialization of girls, young lesbians are less likely than young male homosexuals to assert their sexuality.

Many young women may repress their lesbian sexuality in adolescence and attempt to "pass" as bisexual or heterosexual. Responding to pressures toward conformity which are experienced with special intensity in adolescence, the young lesbian may strive to be the "right kind of girl." Adult protectiveness and surveillance over adolescent females may also discourage the young lesbian's exploration of her sexual identity. The greater restrictions placed upon teenage women, as opposed to teenage men, make it less likely that the young woman who is lesbian or bisexual will be free to explore and locate the local gay community. Typically, lesbian youths are also less likely than young male homosexuals to assert their independence by running away. Thus, many young lesbians are unidentified by others and do not identify themselves.

Internal and external pressures, lack of information and support, family alienation, lead young lesbians and gays into a variety of high risk situations, including substance abuse, familial and peer isolation, and vulnerability to physical and sexual abuse by family members. Inevitably, many of these youths, whether or not they identify themselves as gay, come into contact with the child welfare, mental health, and juvenile justice systems. The staff of these agencies frequently reinforce the same negative or ill-informed reactions of parents of these youth, rooted in the same ignorance, homophobia, and general discomfort with youth sexuality issues. The child welfare workers and juvenile probation officers who are responsible for abused and neglected, delinquent, and status offender children and youth consider them either the victims of parental and familial stress, or the instigator. Similarly, professionals who work with these children will often blame the problems on either parent or child, depending on the circumstances. Blaming one party or the other supports an adversarial view of the parent-child relationship, further polarizing an already damaged relationship. Rather than recognizing the breakdown of communication and understanding in the family system, the child welfare system often repeats the "blaming the victim" dynamic. When workers, in order to "protect" these youth, are not willing to "label" them, the treatment planning, evaluation, and resulting recommendations will reflect denial and perpetuate the covert problems of the client. Willingness to recognize and identify lesbian and gay adolescents may or may not be a controversial issue in itself for social service professionals, depending largely on their personal value systems and the strictures of agency administrations. However, it is now largely acknowledged that throughout the United States, housing and survival needs are not being adequately provided to lesbian and gay youth by the existing youth services agencies.

Presently, child welfare authorities place great emphasis on keeping children in their homes and reuniting children with their families. In the 1970s the problem of runaways was often resolved by placing youth in foster homes, group homes, or institutional settings. This was intended, ideally, to provide respite for and family therapy to the troubled parent and child. Out-of-home care has not worked as intended, largely because of the lack of supportive services directed to the natural parent-youth family. Often these out-of-home placements became long-term placements or failed placements for reasons similar to those which caused the natural family to break down.

Many of these "placement failures" are lesbian and gay youths. Lesbian and gay youth who have been identified or identify themselves as such within youth agencies confront a lack of understanding, an unwillingness to serve, and nonacceptance from foster and group home parents, as well as from workers in crisis shelters and from institutional authorities. Lesbian and gay youth are commonly in the same "hard to place" category as arsonists and suicidal youth. In San Francisco, where one might expect to find optimum availability of services for lesbians and gays, 70 out of 110 youth agencies responded that "they did not have the capacity to serve lesbian and gay youth"[5] on a Delinquency Prevention Commission questionnaire. This means that seven out of eleven agencies contacted by an identified lesbian or gay youth and her or his family will turn them away.

The Need for Alternatives in Working with Lesbian and Gay Youth: A Model

As professionals responsible for these adolescents and their families, we must re-examine traditional support systems and services, and develop appropriate alternatives. Structure, nurturance, and information provision from supportive adults are highly necessary components in any program concerned with the healthy growth and development of youth, including lesbian and gay adolescents.

In cases where gay-sensitive family therapy cannot successfully reunite the family of a lesbian or gay adolescent, finding appropriate out-of-home placement becomes the key issue. Alternative family care for lesbian and gay young people is now a reality in some areas of the United States. Several adult lesbians and gays have brought successful lawsuits, challenging restrictions on their right to become foster or adoptive parents of all children, including lesbian and gay adolescents.[6]

Education of youth-serving professionals is needed in order to raise consciousness about the need for alternative services for lesbian and gay youth, to change homophobic attitudes, and to provide safe environments for youth and families seeking understanding and positive intervention. One example of such an effort is the Sexual Minority Youth Services Coalition (S.M.Y.S.C.),[7] which was organized in San Francisco in 1978 by lesbian and gay professionals working with lesbian and gay youth in a mental health program set up to address the unmet needs of "street youth." Previously, the city government, pressured by the merchants' guild, had responded to the "problem" by providing "clean ups" by the downtown police. The coalition was established to organize and educate the spectrum of agency professionals involved in youth service, and to advocate for services to lesbian and gay youth. From these initial activities, a support network grew which included gay and non-gay youth services professionals and community and youth groups. In addition to advocacy, the coalition provided networking and validation for lesbian and gay professionals involved in all levels of youth services.

Developing alliances with other youth advocacy and human rights groups (e.g., Child Abuse Council, Delinquency Prevention Commission, Legal Services for Children, and the Human Rights Commission) aided the implementation of the initial educational workshops. The coalition provided training, conferences, and workshops to the local Board of Education, Children and Family Services, the Juvenile Justice Commission, community mental health agencies, San Francisco General Hospital, and many other youth and family service agencies in the public and the private sector.

The goals of S.M.Y.S.C. were to develop and monitor services and to influence legislation and other public policy at local, state, and national levels on issues concerning lesbian and gay youth. Additional goals included education and training for the community regarding the rights and needs of sexual minority youth. The methodology used was a combination of education and research, which resulted in documentation of the significant numbers of these youth and families involved in the services systems.

As youth services workers became more comfortable addressing the issues in their agencies, and the administration sanctioned serving these youth, a constituency began to develop. Creating a citywide power base was instrumental in addressing homophobic mythology about the lesbian-gay lifestyle, in proposing recommendations to local and state public agencies regarding appropriate care and treatment of these youth, and in providing youth agencies with the consultation of experts on sex and gender identity.

Once the existence of these youth was recognized and their unmet needs were established through a citywide needs assessment,[8] the issue of housing for lesbian and gay youth emerged as a primary concern. The need for emergency housing, short and long term placements, guardianships, and independent living situations was critically evident. In 1979, S.M.Y.S.C. published a "Housing Report on Attitudes and Availability of Out-of-Home Placements for Sexual Minority Youth."[9] This report dramatically demonstrates the attitudinal impediments to successful placement of these young people. It provided excellent documentation of the state of existing foster homes, group homes, and medical-psychiatric facilities within a 300 mile radius of San Francisco.

The report stressed a frequent dilemma for gay and lesbian runaways. No funding is provided for services to runaways in the city of refuge. By law, the youth is required to return to the city of family residence. It is therefore necessary that lesbian and gay youths be appropriately served within their own counties. This requires that local youth agencies become cognizant of the absence of services and the consequent need for developing local resources. Most important among these are informed family therapy and supportive foster care options. Established ideas about cultural matching have been found applicable to "hard to place" lesbian and gay youth. The report points to strong evidence that placing lesbian and gay youth in nonsensitive heterosexual nuclear foster and group homes repeats the familial dynamic and leads to placement failure.

S.M.Y.S.C. studies also revealed that myths of child molestation, and of "recruitment" by lesbian and gay foster parents, must be directly confronted in order to overcome obstacles to placement of young lesbians and gays in gay-sensitive foster homes. Etiological theories, "phase" theories, and moralistic arguments must emerge in order to be defused and answered, so that practical solutions to the needs of youth who are unwanted and in immediate need of housing and care can be developed. To assure acceptability of lesbian and gay foster parent applicants, licensing agencies were encouraged by S.M.Y.S.C. to do their own recruiting through local lesbian and gay organizations. It is essential, at the outset of such foster care programs, that agencies be assured of high accountability and low liability for such special-need homes.

In addition to the projects described above, S.M.Y.S.C.'s work included extensive networking and advocacy; development and distribution of a pocket-sized directory of local youth resources sensitive to sexual minorities; publication of a brochure of employment information for young gays; sponsorship of cultural events; and presentations of educational workshops for youth-serving agencies.

S.M.Y.S.C. terminated its operations in May 1982, citing "lack of funds, energy, and leadership." During its four years of existence, S.M.Y.S.C. had concentrated most of its attention on issues affecting status offenders (youths charged with acts that are illegal only if committed by a minor) and juvenile prostitution. At the present time, gay and lesbian youth concerns have, in fact, become subsumed under issues relating broadly to status offenders. Specialized resources for gay and lesbian adolescents have been reduced to minimal-level services provided by an inner-city community agency (Hospitality House) and a private crisis shelter (Huckleberry House). In 1983, the Youth Emergency Services Committee (a subcommittee of The Homeless Coalition), with the help of gay political clubs, offered a proposal to the Mayor and the Board of Supervisors which is focused on services to "homeless youth." These services are designed with the primary objective of channeling homeless youth into privately managed shelter, employment, training, and foster care programs, in order to divert them from the juvenile justice system.[10]

It must be noted that the youth addressed by these programs are, in the main, the gay boys who are visible on the streets and are often involved in prostitution. The leadership responsible for continuing efforts on behalf of sexual minorities has become largely male, while the criminal justice focus reflects concern for the gay male youths who, through various avenues, become involved in the juvenile justice system.

The low visibility of lesbian youth is one factor in the limited attention paid to their needs. There are, for example, few self-identified lesbians among the population of street youths. Relatively small numbers are to be found among the membership of gay youth organizations. Adolescent lesbians are not explicitly welcomed into the programs of girl-serving agencies, and they are excluded from some health and welfare programs which serve only young women with family planning needs.

Specific outreach to young lesbians is a critical element in any program of services available to girls. Concern for the needs of lesbian youth, including specialized and supportive family therapy, advocacy, health and gynecological care, must be reflected in the programs of community agencies serving youth. Unless this effort is made, these young women will continue to "fall between the cracks," served neither by agencies for youth/girls, nor by special programs for sexual minority youth which may develop in the future.

Conclusion

The problems of lesbian and gay youth and their families are largely ignored and unrecognized by social service professionals and in community welfare programs. An understanding of the impact of homophobia on lesbian and gay youth and their families is imperative, so that the unique needs of this stigmatized population can be recognized and responded to. Effecting changes in attitudes and beliefs, leading to acceptance, requires education and self-exploration on both institutional and individual levels. Such acceptance, coupled with a better understanding of family dynamics, can lead to the increased availability of information and to the establishing of appropriate gay-sensitive social services which speak to the needs of both lesbian and gay youth.

NOTES

1. Sky Rose, "The Young Lesbian Experience," *Gay Community News,* vol. 1, no. 3, October 1979 (P.O. Box 14412, San Francisco, CA 94114).

2. Robert Vincent Walker, "Our Parents, Ourselves," *Gay Youth Community News,* vol. 2, no. 2, (September 1980).

3. Sexual Minority Youth Service Coalition, Housing Committee, *Housing Report on Attitudes and Availability of Placement for Sexual Minority Adolescents,* 1979.

4. *Counseling Lesbian and Gay Male Youth: Their Special Lives, Special Needs,* edited by Sage Bergstrom and Lawrence Cruz (Washington, D.C.: National Networks Sexual Minority Task Force, 1981). Publication available from New York Runaway Hotline, 2 Lafayette St., 3rd floor, N.Y.C., N.Y. 10007.

5. San Francisco Delinquency Prevention Coordination Council, *San Francisco Youth Needs Assessment,* October 1980 (170 Fell Street, #13, San Francisco, CA 94102).

6. Hayden Curry and Dennis Clifford, *Legal Guide for Lesbian and Gay Couples,* ed. Ralph Warner (Reading, Mass.: Addison-Wesley Publishing Co., 1980).

7. For information, contact: Sexual Minority Youth Services Coalition, P.O. Box 11518, San Francisco, CA 94101.

8. San Francisco Department of Public Health, Center for Special Problems, Community Mental Health Services, *Needs Assessment of Sexual Minority Youth in the City and County of San Francisco,* June 1979.

9. Sexual Minority Youth Service Coalition, *Housing Report.*

10. *Alice Reports* 1 (April 1983), p. 2.

Addictive Love and Abuse:
A Course for
Teenage Women

Ginny NiCarthy

Every kiss, every hug seems to act just like a drug—
You're getting to be a habit with me.
Let me stay in your arms, I'm addicted to your charms—
You're getting to be a habit with me.
I used to think your love was something
That I could take or leave alone,
But now I couldn't do without my supply—
I need you for my own.
Oh, I can't break away, I must have you every day
As regularly as coffee or tea.
You've got me in your clutches and I can't get free,
You're getting to be a habit with me—
Can't break it!
You're getting to be a habit with me.
— Popular song of the 1930s*

The idea persists that "if we can just get to them early enough. . . ." Whoever they are, if we can reach them early, we can "save" them. Save them from the wounds we've suffered, spare them the scars of earlier generations of adult women. That sort of hope was the motivation when Ann Muenchow and I discussed leading a group on battering in an alternative school program for pregnant teenagers.

We decided to offer a course on "Addictive Love and Abuse" because of the close relationship between battering and emotional

---

*You're Getting to Be a Habit with Me," lyrics by Al Dubin, music by Harry Warren, was introduced by Bebe Daniels in the musical comedy film *Forty-second Street,* in 1933.

abuse, and between those two and addictive love. We speculated that although teenage women would hesitate to admit to an interest in battering, they might be attracted to a course related to the subject of love.

Battering and Abuse

In the past seven years it's been well documented that women of all classes, races, ages, and life-styles are physically, emotionally, and sexually abused by men with whom they have intimate relationships.[1] Attempts to estimate the prevalence of violence against women by their intimate partners are limited by the relative secrecy that sill curtains marital and sexual relationships, and are confusing because of the different methods of data collection and varied definitions of each type of abuse. We do know, however, that the annual numbers of abused women are in the millions.[2]

Battering is physical force used by one person against another, to coerce, demean, humiliate, punish, or simply to release tension or demonstrate power. A battered woman is one who has been subjected to battering by her intimate partner on more than one occasion. An abused women is one who has been subjected to physical assault, or emotional abuse, or both, by her intimate partner on more than one occasion.

Since 1971, the questions of why men batter and why women stay with them have been explored by social scientists and feminists. Although this research is still at the beginning stages, some answers have begun to emerge.

Men lash out at their intimate partners for a number of reasons: to release internally or externally imposed tension, which may be the result of overwork, unemployment, financial or health worries, or a myriad of other pressures which are either reality based or simply imagined threats to their self-esteem or well-being; to control their wives and girlfriends; to establish themselves as authority figures by disciplining and punishing their women partners; to prevent women from leaving a relationship.

Whatever the stated or underlying reasons for the urge to lash out, violent men choose their intimate female partners for attack, because the women are available and vulnerable, and because men have society's implicit permission to use violence against their female partners. They can get away with it, without fear of reprisals of the sort that would follow an assault on a colleague, a boss, or a neighbor.

Contrary to popular thinking, there is no such person as *the* battered woman. Although many women develop traits similar to each other after a period of subjection to battering, many different kinds of women become involved with, and remain loyal to, men who beat them, and for a variety of reasons. For some women, the major hold may be love, a commitment to marriage, pressure from family, church, or community, the welfare of the children, or traditional ideas of what a family should be. For others, the most important factors may be economic ties, combined with a fear of the unknown world they will encounter if they leave, a low assessment of their ability to earn a living, lack of skills and education, and emotional dependency. Some women who accept the traditional definition of the man's role as the authority figure and the woman's as obedient wife may fear that defiance of that relationship will cast doubt on their identities as good women and good wives.

Some women are afraid that if they leave, the man will fall apart or commit suicide; they assume responsibility for their husbands' or boyfriends' mental health and physical welfare. Still others remain with abusive men because they fear that if they leave, they or their loved ones will be beaten even more severely than they have been, or even killed, or that their children will be taken from them. These fears are often realistic, based on the male partner's explicit threats. Many abused women have not had a safe place to go, and may remain unaware that special shelters are now available to them in most areas of the country.

Physical battering and emotional abuse are integrally related. Many battering men are masters at using "brainwashing" techniques to control their women: isolating them from others, coercing them into focussing all their attention on the man's needs, degrading and exhausting them. They carry on a campaign to coerce women into becoming dependent, continually demonstrating their self-defined omnipotence and enforcing trivial demands. The occasional indulgences, often as unpredictable as the assaults, provide intermittent reinforcement for staying in the relationships. The hope for change is activated by periodic moments of closeness or other satisfactions, and may be the counterpoint to the longer periods in which the woman feels both hopeless and helpless.

These techniques of emotional abuse are similar to those which have been used to control prisoners of war. (See Appendix I.) The techniques do not have precisely the same effects on people who are not physically locked up (most wives and girlfriends of abusive men are not) as they have on prisoners. However, they are effective methods for any person or group to use in gaining psychological control of another individual or group. As stated in a report published by Amnesty International, these techniques induce "dependency, dread and debility."[3] To the extent that a person is victimized by these techniques, she or he tends to become immobilized by the belief that she or he *is* trapped, *cannot* escape.

When a woman is isolated from everyone except her male partner, her perceptions become distorted. If she is exhausted, threatened, and feels dependent; if she is trained in habits of compliance to the most trivial demands, yet periodically given reason to feel comforted, cared for, indulged, or sexually satisfied—in short, if she has been emotionally abused—she is extremely vulnerable to physical abuse.

Once battering has been introduced as a means of control, it is always an implicit threat in the abuser's demands for compliance, creating a more or less continual feeling of dread. The woman's debility and dependence lead her to believe that battering is inevitable, or even deserved. Thus, physical battering and emotional abuse reinforce each other.

The remarkable thing is that so many women escape from violent men and recover from physical and emotional debility. For many women, the end of isolation from nearly everyone but the abusive partner is the first stage in gaining freedom. A major obstacle in overcoming isolation is the threat of a beating by the partner for any association not approved by him. Other obstacles are the woman's lack of trust in her own judgment, her feeling that no one would want to be with her, fear of change, and guilt feelings for "abandoning" the partner; i.e., acceptance of his view that any "outside" human contact she makes represents abandonment of him. Each of these factors may be caused or exacerbated by the condition of addictive love, which takes different forms depending on whether he, she, or both of them are addicted.

Varieties of Love

Love has been described in many ways, but for purposes of this discussion, it is useful to distinguish among nurturing, romantic, and addictive love relationships.

Nurturing love. Nurturing love incorporates a wish that the beloved person will grow and flourish, developing her/his fullest potential. This in turn implies each partner's openness to the other's deriving nurture from other people and from independent, self-chosen activities and expression.

Nurturing partners encourage each other to enjoy outside relationships and to engage in separate as well as mutual activities. Caring deeply about each other, they are nevertheless capable of relinquishing the relationship, if one or the other wishes to leave it. Freedom from emotional coercion enhances nurturing relationships.

Romantic love. Romantic love implies "rose-colored glasses." Everything about the relationship or the loved one is filtered through a screen that makes it seem perfect. Songs, stories, films, and advertising persuade that there is one person in the universe who is just right for us, and whom we'll know is *the one,* the instant we set eyes on each other. When we think we've found that person, we persuade ourselves that he or she is without flaw. Some unattractive or threatening traits are simply not recognized. Others are re-defined or re-evaluated so that they seem like positive characteristics. "Selfish," "stubborn" or "thoughtless" become "independent," "determined" or "poetically absent-minded." "Possessive" becomes "devoted."

This process is sometimes assisted by the fledgling lovers' determination to put only the best foot forward. Thus, if two people are working hard at presenting themselves as nearly perfect, and at seeing the partner in a similar light, disillusionment must follow when they relax from their poses and lose their romantic visions. In our society at this time, most love relationships probably begin with a romantic view and the characteristic reluctance to be parted from the loved one for even a few moments. The type of relationship that develops over time may depend upon how the couple handles the period that follows the "honeymoon" stage, and whether they persist in promoting unrealistic views of themselves and each other. Not every romantic relationship becomes addictive, of course, but a tendency to addictive love will be supported by a persistent blindness to a partner's flaws.

Addictive love. The couple may be in for serious trouble if one or both believe they can't survive without the other, and the desire to be together every minute develops into the need or demand that the partner be continually available. When these feelings become strongly entrenched, one or both partners may fall into a dangerously addicted condition. *Addicted* implies an urge quite beyond desire. The refrain in the addicted person's mind becomes a variation on "I'll die if he doesn't call me," "I can't live without her," "She's everything to me," "I don't care about anybody but him." Romantic love poems and popular songs provide numerous examples of those sentiments, though in everyday conversation they may be expressed in less histrionic language, especially by people in mid-life and by men.

When men become addicted, they are often adept at hiding it from their partners. Because dependence does not accord with a "manly" image, addicted men are less likely than women to admit to being "hooked." A man may claim that he doesn't need his woman, yet insist that she is treating him badly if she spends time with others, or wants to pursue some independent activities. Even though he feels desperate to hold on to her, he may cover up his dependency by accusing her of being negligent, uncaring, unfeminine and selfish, and by frequent threats to leave her. His demands, expressed in terms of control and criticism, rather than admission of his need, may lead the woman to believe that the problem lies not in his dependence, but in her deficiencies as a caring woman. If she accepts his criticism of her as valid, and believes his assertions that he really doesn't need her, she may feel insecure in the relationship and tend to narrow the focus on her life to concentrate on pleasing him. To the extent that she focuses on his demands and pleasures, she's likely to lose sight of other relationships and activities. This development, along with her fear that her partner may leave her, may contribute to an exaggerated idea of his value and necessity to her life. Thus, she is at risk of becoming addicted to him.

Once the idea takes hold that someone is essential to life, and that nothing else matters, then a series of distortions or suspensions of judgment are likely to follow. Other relationships and activities become expendable. Normally essential pursuits, such as work, education, and avocations become relatively unimportant. The addicted person's vision narrows, the range of emotional, intellectual and interpersonal involvement shrinks. Life then provides so few actual and potential satisfactions that the object of the addiction takes on even more importance, and the addiction increases in severity.

Some of the signs of addiction are:

1.   A conviction that the loved person is needed for survival. Because many men are loathe to admit to this kind of dependence, they may rationalize it in more conventional male terms, such as the belief that the woman must do as she's told, stay at home where she belongs, or make herself available to take care of the man's physical and emotional needs.

2.   A diminishing number of happy, stimulating, interesting, or satisfying experiences with the partner, compared with the time spent in recriminations, apologies, promises, anger, guilt, and fear of displeasing.

3.   A reduction in feelings of self-worth and self-control on the part of the addicted person. This development may manifest itself differently in men and women. In the addicted male, the result may be an accompanying punishment of the presumed cause of his condition, the woman. In the addicted woman, the reduction of feelings of self-worth and self-control may result in depression and increased submission to the man, in the vain hope that she can make things right, thereby regaining some control.

4.   An increasingly contingent way of life. That is, all plans hinge on the partner's availability. If the partner is available, time will be spent with him or her. Other people and activities can be enjoyed only when it's certain that the partner will not be available. Here, too, there are sex differences. A woman may tend to complain about the man's lack of availability, or to wait patiently, fearful that complaints will make things worse; or she may double her efforts to please and

obey, in the belief she can make the man more available by becoming more attractive or compliant. Addicted men may tend to demand availability, acting not as if they need or even want it, but simply as if it's their right, which places their behavior within the norm of many men who are not addicted. This helps them hide their addiction from themselves as well as from the object of their addictive love.

5.   Reduced capacity to enjoy time away from partner. A sense of marking time until the partner is available.

6.   Broken promises, by the addicted person, not to contact the partner as often as has been the case, not to demand an accounting of time or explanations of relationships with other people, not to wait idly for hours in hopes the phone will ring.

7.   A feeling of never being able to get enough of the loved one.

8.   Repeatedly dashed hopes that the next meeting with the loved one will bring more satisfactions than grief.

Addiction and Abuse

Although not all addicted lovers are abused, it is easy to see how an addicted woman may be at risk of abuse. If only one thing or person is of importance or gives the whole of meaning to life, if the addicted woman will do anything to be allowed to have the beloved object, she places herself at his mercy. If the partner is prone to take advantage of her need for him, to the extent of using whatever force is necessary to impose his will, the addicted female may easily become abused or battered.

If the male partner is also addicted, he may be willing to do anything he can think of to stave off the threat of losing love. He may find that name-calling, intimations that the partner is defective as a woman, a sex partner, a mother, or a human being, keep her cowed and willing to do anything to please; but if that seems to fail, or he imagines that she is interested in someone else or that she has rejected him, he may resort to threats or violence, since those are among the principal ways that men learn to control their environment.

It is not, of course, only addicted men who batter and abuse their female partners. As noted above, historically men have been permitted to batter their wives, and have even been legally obliged to control and extract obedience from them, so long as they did not beat them with a weapon "wider than a man's thumb."[4]

Many men persist in the belief that it is their right to discipline their wives, and some women still accept that dictum either as a right belonging to men, or as something that women must endure, in order to have a man at all. Those women who don't accept that men have such a right, or who put limits on it, may either leave the relationship or demand that the man cease his unacceptable behavior. But if the woman is addicted, she fears that any objection she makes will result in her being temporarily rejected, or permanently abandoned, by her partner. Her failure to resist or to leave may be perceived by the partner as permission to continue, and even to escalate his violence, so that whenever he feels a need to release tension or to place blame for his own inadequacies or the conditions of his life, his female partner will be perceived as an appropriate and available target.

Although addicted—and non-addicted—women abuse men, males are generally able to use their superior muscle power and their superior status to intimidate much more successfully than are women. Male and female socialization toward acceptance of their respective traditional roles—the one active and dominant, the other passive and submissive, the man assumed to get on well without a partner, the woman assumed in need of a man—exacerbate the tendency for addicted men to abuse women, and for addicted women to be abused by their male lovers.

Battering and Help for Teenagers

There appears to be more battering by men who are married than those who are not; it frequently occurs when the spouse is pregnant; and there is a strong tendency for it to become more dangerous and more frequent over time. Since teenagers, by definition, have shorter term relationships than most adults, and are less frequently married and pregnant than adults, it has been assumed that battering is less prevalent among the teen population than among adults; and that may be true.

On the other hand, battering may be a greater problem among teens than has been recognized. Certain factors associated with battering—a tendency to romantic-addictive love, low impulse control, low self-esteem and a need to assert control, the female's inability to imagine that she has choices other than to endure punishment—coincide with the situation and characteristics of many adolescents. There is special reason to suspect that battering may be particularly prevalent among pregnant teens.[5]

In one study of four thousand victims of violence by male partners in intimate relationships, the largest group of victims (46 percent) were between twenty-five and thirty-six years old and had children between one and thirteen years old. In over 70 percent of the entire study population, the violence occurred immediately or very shortly after the partnership began.[6] These figures suggest that many of these abusive relationships might have begun in adolescence.

Reaching Teenagers

The battered women's movement has typically reached out to adults, and in many instances shelters and other services have been legally prohibited from serving minors. When young women do avail themselves of the services, they are often six to ten years younger than the women nearest to them in age in the group or shelter. They may feel that they have little in common with the other women, and many may choose not to stay.

Although some shelters for women who are battered have developed programs for children, few have designed educational programs geared specifically to adolescents.[7] The movement against battering has concentrated on education, consciousness raising, practical services, and political or legal activity on behalf of adult women.

Teenaged women are difficult to reach for any service, except through the public schools; and programs that appear to be "psychological" or like "therapy," or which seem to threaten invasions into private lives, are all suspect in the schools. The opportunity to offer such a course as co-leaders was therefore welcomed by Ann and myself, both of us white women with social work degrees and backgrounds in education. Ann is a teacher and counselor in the teen pregnancy program that sponsored the groups, and the author is a private practice specialist in the field of woman abuse.

The Course: Setting, Participants, and Goals

We offered the classes on "Addictive Love and Abuse" under the auspices of a social service agency which provides courses for high school aged women who are pregnant or already parents.[8] The classes took place within the framework of two alternative schools, one predominantly black populated, in the South End of Seattle, one predominantly attended by white students in the North End.

The South End group consisted of young women who were either parents or pregnant. It included one Chicana, one white woman (who attended only two sessions) and eighteen black women. The course began with twelve participants and "shook down," as expected, to six or eight at most sessions. A few came to nearly all the sessions, but most came to six or eight of the fourteen sessions.

The North End group was composed of six or eight "regulars" who came to eight or ten of the twelve sessions, plus another six or eight who attended three or four times. The total included two black women who attended one time and another black woman who attended twice. All of the others are white. Although this group was also sponsored by the teen pregnancy program, only two participants were actually in that program. The others were from the general population at the alternative school.

The age range in each group was fifteen to eighteen. The groups met in classrooms at schools where they were taking other academic classes to gain credits for high school graduation. Our classes were electives and had the attraction of no grades or tests. However, they had to compete with classes that would help students graduate, a goal most students were eager to attain as quickly as possible. We were uncertain whether we could recruit sufficient numbers of students for a lively group, since there was no precedent for a course on battering or other forms of abuse.

Students were recruited by Ann, who was already a teacher

and counselor in the two schools, and by a nurse at one of the schools. They explained to students that "addictive love" would be a core item in our course. A number of students were referred to us by their school counselors, who knew they had been in abusive relationships.

From our experiences in the two groups, we have developed an eight session model for teaching young women about addictive and abusive relationships, the relationships between them, and what can be done to prevent or stop them. Our goals were that the young women would:

1. Become aware of the pervasiveness of violence and abuse in intimate relationships.
2. Recognize signs of addictive love in intimate relationships.
3. Recognize emotional, sexual and physical abuse.
4. Understand the relationship of addictive love to abuse.
5. Understand the roles of power and sex-roles in abuse.
6. Know their rights, including the right not to be abused.
7. Learn about alternatives to emotional abuse, including negotiation, assertiveness, and separation.
8. Learn about helpful resources for battered women, including police, prosecutors and shelters.

Although we did not set it as a formal goal, we also wanted to provide an accepting atmosphere for anyone who chose to talk about her own experiences with battering or abuse or addiction to a man.

The course material that follows has been reorganized somewhat for clarity and ease of presentation. For example, we did not always use the exercises in the sequences presented here; however, we tried them all, plus quite a few others, with varying degrees of success.

In the following pages, I will state the objectives for each session, discuss the exercises we used to reach the objectives, and describe the outcome in one or both groups. (Some exercises were used in only one group.) We are uncertain about the reasons that some exercises had different results in the two groups. Among the important variables between the two groups were ethnicity and the impact of pregnancy or parenting. Readers should take such factors into account, modifying each exercise as seems appropriate to the composition of the group, the setting, and the response leaders elicit as they fit the model to their individual styles.

We sometimes found the fifty-minute class hour a limitation, but we were usually able to complete one or two exercises during each session. The length of time for each exercise varied for each of the two groups. The time you allot will depend on the size and character of your classes.

Session I

EXERCISE I. "BRAGGING."

Objective: Set a tone of informality, acceptance, openness, curiosity.

Leader: "Please tell us your name and something you did in the past week that you feel proud of or good about. It can be a 'brag' about something you did for yourself or something you did for another person.

"Most of us have felt abused by someone—a boyfriend, parent, or teacher—at some time or other, even if we haven't thought of ourselves as an *abused woman*. Sometimes we just feel as though someone is taking advantage of us or exercising too much power over us. When you feel that way, it's a good idea to treat yourself especially well. One way to do that is to give yourself credit for the things you're doing that seem to be right or useful. Making a habit of appreciating yourself is also a good way to keep yourself in a frame of mind that will help you avoid abusive relationships." The leader may either begin the round of "brags" or offer her "brag" when others seem shy or unable to think of anything to say.

The bragging exercise should be used to introduce *each meeting* of the group.

Reactions of South End and North End Groups. Most group members were reluctant to "brag." Even after gentle prodding, only a few responded the first time the exercise was introduced. We continued to open each session with the exercise, and after three or four meetings, nearly everyone participated. Once started, group members looked forward to the exchange of "brags."

EXERCISE II. DEFINING ADDICTIVE LOVE.

Objective: Find out what participants understand by the term "addictive love."

Leader: "We're going to spend some time talking about addictive love today, and I'm wondering whether you've heard the phrase, and what it means to you. You probably know something about drug and alcohol addiction, so perhaps you can imagine what it's like for a person in love to feel that she *has to have* a particular man, or she'll fall apart. How do people feel, and what do they do when they experience addictive love?" As students respond, list their contributions on newsprint. Preserve the lists to use in Session VII, Exercise I.

South End Group. Twelve students attended our initial meeting. It was noisy, chaotic, a confusion of talk and laughter, but the participants were there in far larger numbers than anticipated, and they were enthusiastic about discussing the topic. When we began to talk about addictive love they responded with cheerful recognition: "Oh, you mean 'sprung!' "

In this group we didn't arrive at our anticipated list of the characteristics of being "sprung." The first two traits to be mentioned, jealousy and possessiveness—along with many accompanying complaints about men—were the springboard for such a lively discussion, that we followed the interest of the group and focused on those subjects for the rest of the period.

The most common refrain was, "They expect you to be there for them, but they go out with other women." We discussed various ways to deal with men who cheat. Some suggestions were to act sweet and ignore it; get mad and show it; keep score quietly until a later time, when you can let them have it if they get mad at you for something. No consensus was reached. The group also discussed the question of whether jealousy indicated true caring or not. Participants arrived at a tentative conclusion that it doesn't.

North End Group. In the fashion of alternative schools, students continued to straggle into the classroom throughout the hour, until finally we had fifteen participants. That was too many, and far more than anticipated, but we were pleased at the demonstration of interest.

Students gave these responses to our question of how addicted lovers act and feel:

Can't stand being away from him
Boring
Dependent
With the person for a long time
Hard to break ties

A group member asked, "Why do people think they have to stay in those kinds of relationships?" We turned the question back to the group, and listed these responses from them:

Low self-esteem	Special times hard to give up
Feel worthless	
Deserve bad treatment	Live in the past
Can't get away	First boyfriend
Feel sorry for him	Hard to let go
Need to rescue him	Hope for change

We noticed that most of the reasons given for staying sounded rather negative and asked whether anything positive might keep someone in an addictive relationship. Group members identified closeness and sex as important. They also noted that it's acceptable to have sex with a first boyfriend, but if a young woman breaks up with him and becomes sexually involved with a second boyfriend, her reputation will be spoiled. We then talked about the unfairness of this double standard. Other comments about the difficulty of giving up a first boyfriend were: "He becomes your best friend"; "You lose self-consciousness when you have a boyfriend"; "You feel complete."

The class discussed how "stuck" a woman feels if she gets pregnant, how it adds to her feeling of helplessness and to her fears of separating from the man.

Sessions II and III

These two sessions are described together, because the questions asked of the students may elicit few responses at first, but bring out much richer responses after students have an opportunity to think and talk about the questions between sessions. It may be more useful to do each exercise fairly quickly and then repeat it, filling in whatever blanks there are from the first time around, than to complete each exercise in one session.

EXERCISE I: CONTINUUMS OF ABUSE:
PHYSICAL, EMOTIONAL, SEXUAL.

Objective: Raise awareness of kinds and degrees of abuse.

Leader: "What are some of the ways that men abuse women, physically? Emotionally? Sexually? How do women abuse men?" List answers to each question on newsprint, discussing them in as much depth as seems appropriate and interesting to your group.

Arrange the responses on a continuum for each type of abuse, from less to more damaging. Explain that since opinions of the relative damage of each item may vary, the order of the continuum is, to some extent, arbitrary. Ask students whether you have placed some items toward the wrong end of the continuum. (At the next session, repeating the exercise, ask students for more items, and add them to the continuum.) Point out that there is a tendency for abuse to escalate when the victimized partner seems to accept or cannot stop it in the early stages. Therefore, it's important to notice and stop the seemingly mild abuse when it is first observed. Point out that battering crosses all class and race and life-style lines, that it happens to millions of women each year, and that pregnant women are especially at risk for miscarriages from assaults by violent men.

South End Group. We decided to create a continuum of abuse, by using the students' own experiences, as is often done in adult groups for abused women. We asked what kinds of abuse anyone had experienced at any time in their lives, but the students would not give us direct answers. One or two students, in side comments to friends, hinted at having had such experiences. We asked for clarification of those comments, so that we could use them to make generalizations about the problem, but the students quickly retreated into silence.

We next asked, "Can you think of a time when you felt abused by a parent?" The question brought on a chorus of righteous indignation. "*My* parents would never abuse me!" "*I* would never abuse *my* child!"

In order to get our continuum without intruding into group members' privacy, we tried a more general question: "What are some of the ways that men physically abuse women?" They readily responded, but to our surprise, they simultaneously answered a question we hadn't asked: "How do women physically abuse men?" We listed both sets of responses:

What men do to women	*What women do to men*
Scratch	Scratch
Slap	Slap
Pull hair	Bite
Bend fingers	Pull hair
Sock in arm	Punch
Twist arm	Hit with shoe/broom/stick/
Punch face	pan/umbrella
Black eye	Hit with can opener
Kick in stomach when	Hit with iron
woman is pregnant	Cut with knife
Choke	
Beat up	
Dump out of car	

Some of these items are common forms of abuse one sees or hears about from newspaper accounts and on television. But some, like bending fingers back, men scratching women, and women attacking with can openers and hot irons, have the ring of personal experience or observation. Our general question had allowed group members to begin to speak about the violence in their lives without feeling that they were under personal scrutiny.

This lively group had much to say about the questions we asked about physical, emotional and sexual abuse, but they also liked to move on quickly to new topics. We therefore made short lists of responses to the questions during this session, and returned to them later, adding to each category at the next two meetings, threading the topic into discussions of related subjects.

The first day we dealt with physical abuse, the list supplied by group members included only the first eight items on the "what men do" side. We expressed our surprise at the fact that the women's violence seemed more dangerous than the men's. Class members explained that women had to defend themselves against the superior muscle power of men by using instruments like knives and hot irons. When we returned to the question, there were few changes on the "what women do" side; however, the list of violent acts by men against women became longer, and the items indicated more potential danger.

For the most part, the students thought men and women abuse each other emotionally in similar ways, except for the insulting names each sex typically calls the other.

Emotional abuse of men and women by each other

Yelling
Public humiliation
Telling other people about private affairs
Blaming the partner for own faults
Labelling "crazy," "mess," "stupid," "dumb,"
     "bed-hopper"
Not caring about the other's feelings
Stealing money or coercing the partner into giving it up
Sex-specific name calling:

Women call men	*Men call women*
punk	bitch
dog	dog-bitch
boy	ho (whore)
pussy-eater	tramp
faggot	slut
motherfucker	wench
bastard	wanstitute (wants to be a prostitute)

The group discussed the implication, in many of the negative labels for women, that being highly sexual is unacceptable for a woman, whereas terms which describe men as sexual—e.g., *stud*—are complimentary. The group agreed that there should not be different standards for males and females.

"How do men abuse women, sexually?" was the only one of the three questions asked in this exercise that didn't spontaneously elicit a response about women's abuse of men as well. We asked, "Why is it that women don't sexually abuse men?" The group replied, "Oh, but they do!"

Sexual abuse of women by men	*Sexual abuse of men by women*
Call sexual names	Bite his lip
Jealousy	Pinch/scratch butt
Act indifferent	Bite neck
Threaten to get a new woman	Spit in face
Accuse of being with other men	Kick butt
Calls another woman in front of you	Pull penis
	Kick penis
Always wants to "do it"; gets mad when you don't	Burn with cigarette
	Kick/squeeze balls
Biting, pinching titty	Bite penis
Slaps, pinches to get his way	
Makes woman walk home nude	
Wants sex after hitting you	
Forces sex	
Rape	
Rape with bottles, etc.	
Kills	

North End Group. In response to our questions on ways that men physically, emotionally, and sexually abuse women, items mentioned by students were much the same as in the South End group. This group, however, didn't offer comments about women's abuse of men until we specifically asked about it. Then they listed forms of abuse similar to those mentioned in the South End group.

One difference between the groups was that North End students didn't perceive women as sexually abusive to men. Other differences were a matter of language and style, rather than substance. As an example of these slight differences, here are the North End students' examples of abusive name-calling:

Men call women		Women call men	
bitch	witch	ass	hard-up
evil	sex freak	ass-hole	m.c.p.
slut	prick tease	fucker	numb-nuts
sleazy	scum	hard-headed	fag
whore	cow	pain in the	prick
cunt	low life	ass	

EXERCISE II: EMOTIONAL ABUSE AND BRAINWASHING

Objective: Elicit information about emotional abuse of students by boyfriends and give information about its dangerous impact.

Leader: "We're going to list some types of emotional abuse and we'd like you to give examples of ways that men emotionally abuse women under each of these categories." On newsprint, write these headings with space for filling in examples under each: (1) Enforce isolation of the partner; (2) Insist on attention being focused on their comfort and convenience, and away from the desires of the woman; (3) Make degrading, humiliating comments about the woman or degrading, humiliating demands; (4) Cause exhaustion or feelings of helplessness, incompetence or dependency; (5) Threaten; (6) Demonstrate power or superiority over the woman; (7) Enforce trival demands; (8) Grant occasional rewards or favors.

After students have listed some examples under each heading, explain that the major categories are adapted from a list of methods used in brainwashing prisoners of war. (Appendix I.) Point out that these methods are more or less predictable; they are usually not signs that something is wrong with the person on the receiving end of the treatment.

South End Group. This exercise was not presented in the South End group.

North End Group. Student discussion yielded these examples under the categories we had listed:

Enforces isolation. He "comes on" sexually to your friends, so they stop wanting to be with you. He imagines you're going to pick up somebody everywhere you go. Refuses to take you out. Wants to be with you, always. Questions your other relationships.

Insists the woman's attention be focused on him. He punishes for lack of attention or imagined rejection, so you're continually worried, even obsessed, about being even a minute late when meeting him, about being seen talking to other guys or girls, about looking the way he likes you to look. You ask permission for everything, and soon begin to tell lies about minor things to protect yourself from his punishment.

Makes degrading, humiliating comments or demands. Insists on kinds of sex you don't want. Tells you he's having sex with someone else, flirts with other women when you're right there.

Causes exhaustion, feelings of incompetence, dependency. Presses for information about your activities. Tells you, "I'll take care of you."

Threatens. He says, "I'm going to break up with you, go out with your friends." "I'll kill myself." "I'll expose your secrets to your friends, parents."

Demonstrates power or superiority over the woman. Makes decisions for you. Assumes he knows what's best for you and what you want. Says or implies, "I'm smart; you're stupid."

Enforces trivial demands. Makes you do his wash, get his coffee, dress the way he wants, wear—or not wear—makeup.

Grants occasional rewards or favors. Buys gifts. Takes to movies, or dinner. Gives loving support—especially after he's been mean.

We discussed the tendency of women who are treated in these ways to think that something is wrong with them. We pointed out the importance of overcoming this reaction, of realizing that "I feel humiliated, threatened, isolated, because someone is humiliating, threatening, isolating me."

EXERCISE III. KNOWING WHERE TO TURN FOR HELP.

Objective: Supply information on resources.

Beginning with the second meeting, bring brochures on shelters, safe homes, legal options, counseling services, and other aids to women in crisis and battered women, so that students may pick them up as they feel comfortable in doing so.

For more in-depth information on shelters and safe houses, call the one closest to your community or a women's network that may supply information about shelters. Consider inviting a speaker from one of the shelters to your class. You may also want to invite someone from the police or prosecutor's office.

Each state has different laws, and each community has different ways of carrying out the law. Juvenile offenders are treated differently from adults. You will need to get information about police and judicial response to battering in your community; or you may wish to invite a speaker from the municipal prosecutor's office, a shelter or hot-line for abused women, or some other organization that has expertise on this aspect of the law and how it is applied locally.

Session IV

EXERCISE I. RIGHTS LIST.

Objectives: (1) Raise awareness of individual rights; (2) raise awareness of differences between participants' conceptions of their rights, and the conceptions of rights implied in some male students' explanations of why men batter women.

Ask students to state the rights they believe they're entitled to as students, parents, children or in other appropriate categories. Discuss these rights as you list them on newsprint.

Below is a list of responses to the question, "Why do men batter?" gathered from teenaged males attending an inner-city high school.[9] Post this list for discussion in terms of the rights that have been listed by members of your group.

Why Do Men Batter?
Responses of Some Teenage Males

To establish power over woman

To make sure she doesn't mess up or get the upper hand

For respect

Woman likes it

Getting on man's nerves

Makes man feel good

Man is being used financially

Woman has another man

Woman pushes man with her mouth and attitude

Woman is dishonest

Woman gives man a disease

Self-defense; woman hits first

Misunderstanding

Flashbacks

South End Group. We asked students to think about and state their rights—as women, as students, as parents, as children, as blacks, as people. They told us they have the right to:

Have a home

Speak out

See friends

Talk on the phone

Go out

Not be discriminated against on the basis of race

See family members

Not be a slave to anyone

Good health

Go to school

Fail in school

Keep our children

Use birth control

Have an abortion

Have enough money to survive

As part of a couple, or specifically in relation to men, they claimed the right to:

Be open and honest with each other

Express feelings without punishment

Spend time together

Refuse sex when it isn't wanted

Have a good sex life, the way you want it

We next discussed the "Why Do Men Batter?" list supplied by male high school students. Our students were outraged by most of the "reasons" high school men listed for male battering. The one notable exception was in respect to venereal disease, which students thought might deserve physical punishment. We discussed the men's list in terms of the rights it implied the men thought were reasonable, compared with our group's list.

North End Group. This group arrived at a rights list that was similar to the South End group's list. In response to the list of explanations by high school men of why men batter women, they voiced ideas similar to those of the South End students, including righteous indignation at the idea of a woman giving a man a disease.

Susie commented, "That woman should have her legs broken!" Although no one else offered such an extreme reaction, the group seemed, at least, to assent silently to her anger. We suggested that a man who believed he'd been given a disease by his girlfriend would do well to ask some questions of her before determining he'd been betrayed. We suggested that a well-meaning person could make an honest mistake in transmitting a disease (which might have been contracted before the relationship began, for instance).

We suggested that the man's punishment of the woman might not get him what he wanted at all, and that an assault on the woman very likely would make things worse, even from his point of view. We had no success in persuading Susie that vengeance offers limited satisfactions, but we were at least able to move the group from a generally punitive stance to some degree of interest in a problem-solving approach.

EXERCISE II. NEGOTIATION AND ASSERTIVENESS:
DISCUSSION AND ROLE PLAYS.

Objectives: (1) Help students recognize the difference between choosing to give up rights and having them taken away; (2) practice negotiating for rights, when a partner doesn't recognize them.

Leader: Discuss situations in which one might choose to give up one's right as part of a compromise, or because at a particular moment it isn't of great importance to exercise it, and the difference between giving it up and having it taken. Include brainstorming of the various reasons why it's sometimes difficult to exercise rights (fear of angering a partner, or of losing him) and what a woman can do if her man steps over boundaries, infringing on her rights.

Leader: "What can you do, if your boyfriend. . . .?" On the basis of what students have said about the rights they've just listed, or previous discussions, choose for discussion the problem that seems most common for members of your group. Without attempting to reach agreement on which ideas are best, ask students for suggestions of what to do and say when a man refuses to recognize a woman's rights. Encourage students to develop their individual standards and styles of negotiations.

Move from the discussion to role playing. Leaders demonstrate an assertive response to a boyfriend's attempt to abrogate his partner's rights. If there is only one leader, she can play the young woman and enlist the help of a student to play the boyfriend. The leader first plays the young woman assertively standing her ground. The role play can then be repeated with the variation that the young woman holds to a certain line, but offers some amount of compromise ("I won't give up my friends, but I'm willing to spend Friday and Saturday nights with you"). Leaders should emphasize that compromise is very good and useful in relationships, when it is *willingly* given, but that it becomes submissiveness if it's coerced or forced. The person in the young woman's role should not offer the compromise unless she really wants to, and she will be more confident of that decision if she decides what she's willing to give *before* the discussion with her boyfriend. During the role play, she can ask for time to think about it by herself before agreeing to anything. If she does that in a real situation, it will help her to be certain she hasn't been manipulated or frightened into giving in, only to regret later that she gave up an important right.

Leader: "We're going to demonstrate how you can talk to someone who may be treating you badly, without being hostile yourself, and without giving in. I'm going to play the young woman being mistreated by my boyfriend, and I'll try to say how I feel, what I want, and what I'm willing to do, with respect for him and for myself, and without giving up my principles. He may decide to go along with the idea or not, but I will probably feel better about myself, at least, if I stick to what I know is right for me, and don't stoop to his level of manipulation and disrespect. I've asked Jane to play the boyfriend, and to try to do everything she can think of to intimidate me or make me feel guilty, or scared of losing him."

After the role play, do a self-evaluation in terms of the things you said you'd try to do. Then ask the "boyfriend" to say how "he" felt in the role, at various times during the exchange. Ask whether there was anything you might have done differently that might have caused a change in him. Then open the discussion for comments from other class members.

South End Group. This exercise was not presented in the South End group.

North End Group. Ann and I played a young woman defending her right to see her friends, and a boyfriend refusing to "allow" it. The first time, the boyfriend came around to the woman's point of view and agreed that it was her right to see her friends. We played it again with the boyfriend threatening to break up the relationship, and following through when she held her ground.

The discussion that followed indicated that students could hardly imagine risking losing the relationship, even though they thought the boyfriend wasn't worth holding on to.

We next asked that two students do a similar role play. We had difficulty getting volunteers. When two reluctant volunteers took on the roles, they felt uncomfortable and had difficulty thinking of what to say. We asked other students to feed them lines, which the players picked up as they seemed useful. With this approach, almost everyone participated in some way, and all had an opportunity to imagine what they might say, and how they would say it, in a similar situation.

Session V

EXERCISE I: FILM AND DISCUSSION.

Objectives: (1) Create empathy for women in abusive situations; (2) show how shelters and safe homes can help abused women; or, depending upon the content of film (3) explain legal options.

Show a film of your choice on battering (see Bibliography). We used two films, both of them excellent. If these films are not readily available to you, you may wish to choose others, perhaps including a film particularly relevant to your location or your population. It is advisable to choose a film that is no more than forty minutes long—thirty is better for a one-hour class—and to start it as soon as the class hour begins, regardless of whether or not all the students have arrived. If the film is good, it is likely to provoke an emotional response; you'll therefore need at least twenty minutes for students to express their reactions, discuss them, and recover a bit from the emotional impact.

Some useful questions are, "What do you think she should have done at . . . point?" "How do you think she felt?" "What would you do if . . . ?" "What would have happened . . . ?" However, a film about battered women may elicit any number of unpredictable responses, so allow time for discussing the feelings and thoughts that may be important to students, as well as for the discussion questions you prepare.

South End Group. We showed the film, *A Family Affair,*[10] about a woman who is beaten by her husband, some of the effects on their child, and the ways in which the law operates to help the woman. Comments during the film were mostly to the effect that "I'd kill him."

After the film Maria talked about the father of her child, whom she'd had to marry because it's "the Mexican way." Chrystal seconded that idea (and we later learned that she too was involved with a Mexican man who beat her). Maria described at length her troubles with her husband, his physical abuse of her, and the difficulties of getting a divorce. The phrase "the Mexican way" was threaded throughout as an explanation for battering and the pressure to marry when pregnant. The rest of the group listened intently to the story of this real, live Battered Woman in their midst.

When we could get a moment's attention we pointed out that battering is not the "way" of Mexicans any more than of whites or blacks, that it cuts across all class and race lines, and as far as anyone knows seems to happen to all kinds of people.

Cheryl talked about a recent fight she's been in with the best friend of her baby's father. The friend is gay, and Cheryl believed he was after her man. When she attacked him, the police came, but decided that the incident was "petty." They did not arrest her. Telling the story to the class, Cheryl laughed and bragged a bit. "He won't mess with me. He knows how crazy I am. I would kill him."

The film, followed by Maria's and Chrystal's stories, created a mood of excitement. The babble of talk suggested that the class saw killing a violent, troublesome man as a sensible and effective way of dealing with him. Students observed that the deed can be done when the man is asleep, and that the woman will probably "get off on self-defense." It was hard to tell whether the apparent consensus was real, or whether it was mostly the opinion of a few students with loud, enthusiastic voices. Class ended before we had an opportunity to find out, so we made a note to bring the topic up again. (We needn't have worried. It came up again and again.)

North End Group. We showed the film *No Longer Alone,*[11] which centers on the experiences of several women in a shelter, and shows how shelters and safe homes help battered women. The protagonists are real women in real crises, their bruised faces and bodies giving testimony to their experience. The pain of their situations is movingly conveyed. After the film, the group sat in tearful silence.

Finally, Susie broke the silence, sounding angry, frustrated, almost desperate. "Don't they ever fight back?" she blurted out.

Marion spoke up soberly. "I did. I broke his nose."

There was another silence. Perhaps we were all adjusting to the idea of this petite, pretty teenager breaking a man's nose. One of the leaders asked, "Would you like to talk about what you did and how it worked out for you?" Marion became tearful but she was glad to talk about socking her violent boyfriend. It made him stop hitting her long enough for her to escape. She thinks it was the right thing to do, as was calling the police, although she expressed some sadness about his having gone to jail for assaulting her. (He had been charged with other offenses and was already on parole.)

We discussed the option of calling police and the possibility of jail sentences under various circumstances. We gave out packets of information which are available from our state Department of Social and Health Services, on how to use the justice system in cases of assault by intimate partners. Students asked questions about relief and protection available to victims of battering. This gave us an opportunity to make a general distribution of literature on local shelters, counseling groups, and other resources.

Session VI

EXERCISE I: THE BURNING BED

Objectives: (1) Broaden students' views of women's options in abusive and potentially abusive situations; (2) help students recognize possible consequences of specific choices.

Read a short selection from *The Burning Bed*[12] to the class. This is the true story of a woman who endured many years of battering and emotional abuse from her husband, and who finally set fire to him while he slept, burning him to death. Brainstorm as many ideas as possible of what the woman could have done in her specific situation. Then ask, "What would be the best or right thing to do?" "What would be the likely consequences of each?" "How might the woman feel after carrying out her choice?"

Depending upon how verbal your class is, which will affect the length of discussion, you may want to select for discussion critical incidents from several stages of the woman's life, e.g., her meeting with her future husband as a teenager (pp. 47–49); occasions when she's just been beaten (pp. 59, 113–155) and when her husband has refused to let her work or go to school (pp. 135–138; 175–181); and shortly before and after she kills her husband (pp. 182–185; 188–190).

Although the woman who "burned the bed" felt that she had no other choice than to kill her husband, you can focus the discussions so that students are able to see that different choices at earlier points in her life would have spared her that tragic final decision.

Students may be impressed the the righteousness of the woman's choice, and reassured that she "got off" and was spared a jail sentence. They may need help in focusing on the emotional consequences for her and her children of killing the man who was her husband and her children's father.

South End Group. As an alternative to *The Burning Bed,* students read, in class, an eighteen page story (which actually took two class hours, with discussion), from an unpublished work of the author, about Maddie, a black woman who was molested at the age of three, beaten by her father, and subsequently by the boyfriend by whom she became pregnant at fifteen. She married him at sixteen, and after ten years of being battered, left him to make a satisfying independent life for herself and two children. (You may want to use a short story appropriate to the ethnic composition of your class.)

The details about Maddie's early childhood provoked an animated discussion of child abuse and molestation—and more talk of retribution by killing. Rose: "I'd kill anyone who molested my three-year-old." Maria, speaking of her abusive father: "I wanted to kill him, to put a knife to his stomach when he was sleeping, but I couldn't do it. I didn't have enough nerve." Rose, apparently referring to any adult who abused or molested a child: "I'd tie him up when he was sleeping and beat him."

We were unsuccessful at persuading students to think through the ramifications of killing as a solution.

Students asked to role-play a part of Maddie's story: Maddie has left work to come home at lunchtime to tell her husband how much she enjoyed their anniversary celebration the night before. She surprises him with another woman. In our discussion of the situation before the role-play, at least three students were adamant about punishing the other woman, rather than the man. To everyone's surprise, in the role-play the two women developed friendly feelings for each other.

In the discussion that followed students decided that the man was at fault, not necessarily the other woman, after all. Some thought Maddie should retaliate against her husband in some way. Most thought she should leave him.

North End Group. Students were immediately caught up in the story of *The Burning Bed.* They were appropriately horrified at the burning and wished that the woman had made some earlier choices to avoid the situation that developed. They thought she shouldn't have continued dating her future husband in high school, though they could understand easily why she did. Most of them were adamant in their beliefs that the woman should have defied the husband and gone out to work and to classes when she wanted to.

EXERCISE II. FOCUSSING ON FEELINGS.

Objective: Help students realize possible consequences of specific choices in abusive situations.

Read the following excerpts from the coroner's report aloud, to illustrate that many women kill their spouses and are killed by them, in situations where it may be unplanned and later regretted:

"Sixty-five years old. Black. Shot by her husband after altercation. She stabbed him in right arm and he shot her in chest."

"Twenty-one years old. Caucasian. Deceased's estranged husband came over. Deceased called police. Police found no male. Husband returned, victim shot him in arm and he shot and killed her."

"Fifty years old. American Indian. He began to hit her with fists. She got hunting knife and stabbed him. She is in jail."

After you have read the reports, allow a little time for students to express their feelings, then ask them to relax and focus on their feelings.

Leader: "Shut your eyes for a moment, and relax. Breath in and out, quietly. Focus on your breath going slowly in and out. . . . Imagine that the man you love is hitting you. . . . Without planning it at all, you reach for something you can use to fend him off. . . . He slumps to the floor. . . . He looks as though he might be badly hurt. . . . Then, you realize that you've killed him. . . . Picture him dead. . . . Imagine yourself explaining to people he knew and people you know that you killed him. . . . If he was the father of your child, imagine explaining to your child how you came to kill him. . . . Let yourself experience the feelings. . . . Sit with those feelings. . . . I'll count to one from five, and when I get to one, let yourself slowly come back to the here and now, as slowly or as quickly as you like. . . . Five . . . four . . . three . . . two . . . one. . . ."

South End Group. The combination of hearing about the deadly consequences of violence and having an opportunity to experience the feelings they might have about killing was effective in helping students to project their reactions of sorrow, and to get beyond the righteous anger that had previously made killing appear to be an acceptable solution to abuse. It allowed them to think about the moral, legal, emotional, and social consequences of killing a loved one.

The class discussed ways of preventing anger from reaching the point at which there is danger of a lethal act. We suggested calling the police at the first sign that anger may lead to violence, but that idea was greeted with considerable skepticism about the efficacy of police response. Our explanations of the recent tightening of state law and subsequent improvements in local police procedures did not appear to put a dent in students' distrust of the police.

North End Group. This exercise was not presented in the North End group.

EXERCISE III. FINISH THE STORY

Objective: To consider choices and their consequences in a variety of abusive situations.

We wrote several uncompleted one- and two-paragraph stories and asked students to write endings for them in class. You may decide to write your own stories, which specifically address the situations of your population, or to use the stories below.

Some students may complete all four stories, some may struggle to complete one. When all students have completed at least one story, ask for volunteers to read the completed story, or if they are too shy, to tell the ending to the group. Use the following questions as aids in discussing the characters and their actions:

"Who is responsible for . . . ?"

"At what point might one of the characters have done something different that would have given the story a different ending?"

"Is the story really finished?"

"Are the actions of the characters right in a moral or ethical sense?"

"How would each character feel at the end of the story?"

Finish This Story

Read the unfinished stories below. Choose two stories to complete. Write the endings as you think they might happen in real life.

I

Tyree is eighteen years old. He dropped out of school at sixteen. Although he says he's going to get his G.E.D., he keeps putting it off. One evening, he finally goes off to a G.E.D. class. On the way he meets a buddy, they stop for several beers, and Tyree never gets to class.

Christal, the mother of Tyree's child, has spent the day at school, and most of the evening trying to comfort a teething baby. She's just gotten the baby to sleep when Tyree comes in, a bit drunk, loud, and wanting sex. She is not in the mood. She says, "Take your hands off me! I've been working all night, cooking dinner, doing dishes, taking care of the baby, and what have *you* done?"

He says, "Oh, come on, baby, have some fun. A man has to go out now and then to relieve the tension. Loosen up a little. I'll go to the damned class next week."

Christal: "What? You didn't even go to *class* before you got drunk? You're never going to amount to anything. You're just a bum, Tyree. . . ."

Tyree hits her on the head with his open hand.

_____

_____

_____

_____

_____

II

Jane and Carl have lived together for a year. She is getting more and more disgusted with him for not working and for taking the money she earns for marijuana and wine. She's not sure whether she stays with him because she's still in love, or because she wants to remain with the father of her child.

She recently met Sam, who has a good job, and who really seems to appreciate her. One Saturday afternoon she goes to his apartment to borrow a tape, and before she knows it, she's in bed with him. Carl suspects she's betraying him and follows her. When she leaves Sam's apartment, Carl grabs her and pushes her into his car. Gunning the motor, and with a squeal of tires, he speeds away.

_____

_____

_____

_____

_____

III

Bob has a low-paying job as a grocery store cashier. The boss says that if he works hard, he'll be an assistant manager in five or ten years. He works long, irregular hours at the store, while Mary works at home, taking care of their sons, ages one and three years. Mary is busy, but often bored. She doesn't even have enough money to take a bus to her friend's house.

She looks forward to Bob's coming home, so she can talk to him. One night, when he hasn't come home by nine, she turns on the T.V. At ten, he comes in. Mary looks up from the commercial and says, "Hi! How was your day?"

Bob starts off on a long story about an argument he had over the price of soup, and Mary wishes she hadn't asked. She turns back to the last act of her T.V. movie.

Bob, who is usually good-natured, snaps off the T.V., saying, "I work hard all day! At least you could show some respect and listen to me when I come home!"

Mary says, " _You_ don't respect _me_! You come home whenever you feel like it, don't even bother to call, and expect me to jump up to attention. And it's the same boring stuff every night. The price of canned peas! Who cares? I'd rather watch T.V., and you have no right to just turn it off."

Bob answers, "Oh, yes I do. I pay the bills around here, and you wouldn't even _have_ a T.V. if it weren't for me." He grabs her, and pulls her out of her chair. She slaps him.

_____

_____

_____

_____

_____

IV

Matt and Sadie have been going together for about
a year. They had a fight about money, and Matt decides
he's going to get back at Sadie for some things she said.
He asks an ex-girlfriend to have coffee with him. They
sit right at the window table of the local hang-out and
hold hands and make eyes at each other. Sadie walks by
with a woman friend, just as Matt thought she would.
Matt pretends he doesn't see her, but she sees him, all
right, with the other woman, and _____

_____

_____

_____

_____

South End and North End Groups. Both groups enjoyed
writing the endings and discussing the probabilities of their
happening. There were lively discussions and disagreements on all
the questions. We collected the stories, and at the beginning of the
next session summarized the group's endings to each story.

Besides the "Finish This Story" exercise, we made up and
read a "story" to the North End group: The boyfriend of a teenaged woman passes out at a party. Upon waking up, he finds his
date "slow-dancing" with another partner. He is furious and hits
her.

Our intention in reading the story had been to make the point
that the person who gets drunk and violent is responsible for his
condition and therefore for his acts. We didn't foresee that the
woman's "slow-dancing" would be viewed by the class as a very
serious offense, and would skew the responses to the story. Our
students thought that even though the boyfriend had deserted his
date by passing out, she had no right to "slow-dance" with some-

one else. Some thought she shouldn't have danced with anyone at all, slow or fast. On the supposition that this was the first time the man had behaved badly (the story didn't say) there was more sympathy for the man than the woman.

We asked, "What would you have done?" The answers: "I wouldn't have danced." "I would have taken the boyfriend home." "I would be understanding and listen." Susan: "She still wants to be with him, after all. And it wasn't very bad." Harriet (who had been beaten by her boyfriend): "I would leave." Susie: "But you didn't." Harriet: "I learned the hard way."

After group, Sheila told one of the leaders that she had just broken up with her boyfriend because he hit her. He had been violent before, and she thought they would get back together later, but was proud of making him stay away for a time. (Later, we heard she had a new boyfriend.)

Session VII

EXERCISE I. ADDICTIVE LOVE, ABUSE, AND BATTERING: DISCUSSION OF RELATIONSHIPS BETWEEN THEM

Objectives: To recapitulate major points about the relationships between addictive love and abuse and battering.

Put up newsprint sheets on addictive love and emotional abuse from Session I, Exercise II and Sessions II and III, Exercises I and II. Leader: "What do you see as the relationship between addictive love, emotional abuse, and battering? In our first session, this is how the group described addictive love, and later you said these are the ways that men abuse women. What are some of the ways that one might lead to the other? What are some of the things that might cause emotional abuse to escalate into battering?" If students don't see the connections, explain them yourself, referring, if necessary, to pages 116 to 123 of this article.

South and North End Groups. Both groups understood the relationships quite well, and were concerned about how to stay out of potentially damaging relationships.

EXERCISE II. IDENTIFY ADDICTIVE LOVE

Objective: Help students recognize early signs of addicitve love.

Ask students what some of the first signs of addictive love

might be. List them on newsprint. Ask for suggestions on what to do when one notices those signs. Write the suggestions next to each of the early signs.

After you have listed students' suggestions, add any of the following options which have not been brought up:

1. You can end the relationship.

2. If you *act* as if you're not addicted by continuing to see other friends, engaging in sports, doing well in school, there's a chance you can stop the addiction.

3. Ask yourself what's missing in your life that makes you feel that you "have to have" this man. Search for other ways to meet these needs.

South and North End Groups. We cannot report on the classes' responses to this exercise, inasmuch as we presented it piecemeal, as the issues arose in the midst of other exercises. We believe that the exercise should be presented as a distinct unit, in the sequence suggested here.

Session VIII

EXERCISE I. GUARDING AGAINST ABUSE

Objective: Reinforce awareness of ways of recognizing potentially addictive and abusive relationships.

Using the list of questions below, from the book *Getting Free,* ask students to answer as many as possible, quickly, while they're thinking of a current boyfriend, or a past one, or one they'd like to date. Leader: "Just answer the question as quickly as you can, giving your first impressions, even if you are uncertain of them. If you don't have enough information about this man to answer some of the questions now, you might want to pay close attention to his behavior and conversation for clues. Depending upon your relationship with the man, you might even decide to give him the questions to answer about himself."

*Questions to Ask Yourself About a New Man**

1. Can you state particular characteristics of his that you love? .... _____
2. Can you give examples of them? .... _____
3. How many essential characteristics of your "ideal man" does he have? .... _____
4. Does he accept your right to decide if you'll use birth control? .... _____
5. Does he think it's a wife and mother's right to decide whether to work at a paid job? .... _____
6. Is he willing to have you spend time alone, even if he'd like to be with you? .... _____
7. Is he glad you have other friends? .... _____
8. Is he pleased at your accomplishments and ambitions? .... _____
9. Does he think women can and should be as wise, worldly confident, strong, decisive, and independent as men? .... _____
10. Does he sometimes ask your opinion? .... _____
11. Does he both talk and listen? .... _____
12. Does he tell you when his feelings are hurt? .... _____
13. Does he think it's okay for men to show they're weak or vulnerable and to cry sometimes—aside from right after he's abused you? .... _____
14. Is he able to express affection aside from the times he's sorry for abusing you and when he wants, or you're having sex? .... _____
15. Are there some special traits about women (ability to express emotions, willingness to be vulnerable) that he admires? .... _____
16. Does he like and admire his mother or sister? .... _____
17. Does he have good friends? .... _____
18. Does he have interests besides you? .... _____
19. When angry does he break or throw things? .... _____
20. Does he lose his temper suddenly over small things, especially when he doesn't perform as well as he'd like? .... _____
21. Does he ask you about other men in your past life? .... _____
22. Does he want to know where you've been when you've been out? .... _____
23. If you stay out late, does he insist on an explanation? .... _____
24. Does he believe husbands should make the important decisions? .. _____

*From *Getting Free: A Handbook for Women in Abusive Relationships*, by Ginny NiCarthy. Copyright ©1982 by Ginny NiCarthy. Reprinted by permission of the author and The Seal Press.

25. Does he think there are any circumstances in which it's okay for a man to hit a woman (for instance, if he finds "his woman" with another man)?. . . . . _____

26. Is he jealous of your friends or relatives? . . . . _____

27. Does he think you're with another man if you're not home when he calls?. . . . . _____

28. Does he think you're going to "cheat" on him when you talk to a man or dance with an old friend? . . . . _____

29. Does he think men should earn more than women? . . . . _____

30. Does he especially want boy babies and associate fathering boys with masculinity? . . . . _____

31. Does he think you have enough education, even though you want to go to school? . . . . _____

32. Does he get angry if meals are late, or the food isn't just right?. . . . . _____

33. Does he have the traits that often "hook" you into involvements with abusive men? . . . . _____

34. Does he take over when you're having trouble doing something, whether you want him to or not? . . . . _____

35. When he's hurt, does he act angry instead? . . . . _____

36. Does he silently sulk when angry?. . . . . _____

37. Does he drink or take drugs almost every day or go on periodic binges? . . . . _____

38. Does he ridicule you for being stupid or for characteristics that are "typical of women"?. . . . . _____

39. Do you like yourself less than usual when you've been with him? . . . . _____

40. Has he spent time in jail?. . . . . _____

41. Was he abused as a child? . . . . _____

42. Does he sometimes put you on a pedestal, saying he doesn't deserve you? . . . . _____

43. Are there some qualities you especially like about yourself that he disapproves of or ridicules? . . . . _____

44. When you've acted independently, has he sometimes called you a "women's libber" or "dyke"? . . . . _____

45. Has he been in fist fights or hit other women he's been involved wtih?. . . . . _____

"No" answers to questions among the first eighteen indicate potential trouble. When students have answered most of these eighteen questions, ask if they have any "no" answers that trouble them. Ask whether they believe that some of the "no" answers are *not* indicative of potential abuse. Encourage students to argue their points.

Give students an opportunity to answer the rest of the questions. When a few of them have finished, ask them whether they'd be willing to walk away from a relationship in which the answers were "yes" to those questions. If so, which ones, or how many "wrong" answers would be necessary to make them leave? Which of them seem unimportant to them?

Encourage students to take copies of the questionnaire with them for their reference, when they become involved with a new man.

South End Group. We did this exercise very briefly, because a topic pressing to our participants took precedence: how could students help a friend who was in an abusive relationship? The class discussed whether friends should volunteer to help and how far they should go in rescuing an abused friend. The two students who were most concerned and compassionate had been in battering relationships themselves.

North End Group. The discussion of the questions from *Getting Free* was lively, and could have continued for several sessions. We also discussed the value of paying attention to somatic symptoms—tightness in the chest, stomach aches, headaches—and focussing on them long enough to determine what they may mean. Somatic symptoms may indicate anger, hurt, or humiliation that isn't being recognized. Such feelings may need to be expressed or diminished through making changes in a relationship. The group understood that shrugging aside these symptoms and feelings as if they do not matter may be to ignore important information that is needed to make decisions.

EXERCISE II. EVALUATION OF GROUP SESSIONS

Objective: To provide feedback for leaders and group members.

Hand out evaluation sheets (see Appendix II). Give students about ten minutes to fill them out before collecting them. Ask students if there are some things they'd like to say about the group—what they liked, would like more of, wish we had or had not done—and let them know their comments will be useful in any future offerings of the course.

South and North End Groups. Because our attendance at

the last groups was low, we obtained few evaluations, though we were able to get a few from absent members, by tracking them down in their other classes. All of the respondents' comments were positive, and typically stated, in writing and orally, that they wished the course could continue and that we could discuss more topics. They agreed that this was a nearly unique opportunity to talk openly about the things that were of great importance to them. These comments accorded with others that were offered spontaneously during several sessions.

CLOSING COMMENTS.

Because many students may feel, as ours did, that the sessions have been beneficial, and may regret their ending, leaders may wish to suggest that the close of the course needn't represent an ending. Leader: "In a way, the ending of this group is a beginning. Some of you will see each other from time to time, and even though you may not become friends, you'll have a kind of common language from this group. You can continue using the insights learned in the group, and its common language, among yourselves and with other women in the future."

CLOSING EXERCISE: BRAG.

Ask each student to mention something she liked about the way she participated in the group.

Appendix I

Biderman's Chart of Coercion*

General Method	Effects (Purposes)
1. Isolation	Deprives victim of all social support of his ability to resist
	Develops an intense concern with self
	Makes victim dependent upon interrogator

---

*From Amnesty International, *Report on Torture* (London: Gerald Duckworth, 1973), p. 49. A third column, headed "Variants," is omitted here.

2.	**Monopolisation of perception**	Fixes attention upon immediate predicament; fosters introspection
		Eliminates stimuli competing with those controlled by captor
		Frustrates all actions not consistent with compliance
3.	**Induced debility Exhaustion**	Weakens mental and physical ability to resist
4.	**Threats**	Cultivates anxiety and despair
5.	**Occasional indulgences**	Provides positive motivation for compliance
		Hinders adjustment to deprivation
6.	**Demonstrating 'omnipotence'**	Suggests futility of resistance
7.	**Degradation**	Makes cost of resistance appear more damaging to self esteem than capitulation
		Reduces prisoner to 'animal level' concerns
8.	**Enforcing trivial demands**	Develops habit of compliance

Appendix II

Evaluation

Was this class mostly:

Boring			**Okay**		**Interesting**	
1	2	3	4	5	6	7

What did you like most?

What did you not like about it?

What new understandings or knowledge or feelings do you have as a result of the class?

If you were advising a teacher who was planning another class like it, what would you leave out or add or change?

NOTES

1.   Murray A. Straus, Richard Gelles, and Suzanne K. Steinmetz, *Behind Closed Doors: Violence in the American Family* (New York: Anchor Books/Doubleday, 1981), pp. 123–152; Lenore E. Walker, *The Battered Woman* (New York: Harper and Row, 1979), pp. 21–23; Diana E.H. Russell, *Rape in Marriage* (New York: MacMillan Publishing Co., 1982), p. 17; pp. 185–189.

2.   Del Martin, in introduction to Jennifer Baker Fleming, *Stopping Wife Abuse* (New York: Hawthorn Books, 1978), p. 10; Murray A. Strauss, "Wife Beating: How Common and Why?", *Victimology: An International Journal* 2, 3–4 (1977–78), p. 443.

3.   Amnesty International, *Report on Torture* (London: Gerald Duckworth, 1973), p. 45.

4.   R. Emerson Dobash and Russell Dobash, "Love, Honor and Obey: Institutional Ideologies and the Struggle for Battered Women," *Contemporary Crisis: Crime, Law and Social Policy* 1 (June–July 1977), pp. 403–415.

5.   Richard J. Gelles, *The Violent Home* (Beverly Hills, Calif: Sage Publications, 1974), pp. 145–146.
Violence between dating teenage partners may also be more common than has heretofore been suspected. According to a recent study of 256 high school students, conducted by Women Escaping a Violent Environment, 27 percent of those interviewed reported some form of violent dating behavior. "Girls were equally as violent as boys," but were.more likely to be victims of serious injuries. *The Tribune*, San Diego, June 16, 1983; and the *Seattle Post–Intelligencer*, June 30, 1983.

6.   Maria Roy, *The Abusive Partner: An Analysis of Domestic Battering* (New York: Van Nostrand Reinhold Co., 1982), p. 34.

7. · A.W.A.R.E. shelter for battered women is one of the few that has developed an educational curriculum for high school students. For information, write to A.W.A.R.E., Attn. Rosemary Murray, Box 809, Juneau, Aka. 99802.

8.   Medina Children's Services and New Beginnings Shelter for Battered Women, both of Seattle, were sponsors of the course.

9.   The list was done as an exercise in a special session on battering led by the author.

10.   See Bibliography.

11.   *Ibid.*

12.   *Ibid.*

Bibliography

BOOKS

Dobash, R. Emerson and Russell. *Violence Against Wives: A Case Against Patriarchy*. New York: The Free Press, 1979.

Fleming, Jennifer Baker. *Stopping Wife Abuse*. New York: Anchor Books/ Doubleday, 1979.

Martin, Del. *Battered Wives*. San Francisco: Volcano Press, 1981.

McNulty, Faith. *The Burning Bed*. Bantam: New York, 1980.

NiCarthy, Ginny. *Getting Free: A Handbook for Women in Abusive Relationships*. The Seal Press (310 So. Washington St., Seattle, Washington 98104), 1982.

Peele, Stanton. *Love and Addiction*. New York: Signet Books, 1975.

Walker, Lenore E. *The Battered Woman*. New York: Harper and Row, 1979.

JOURNALS

Victimology: An International Journal. "Stop Abuse." vol. 2, nos. 3–4, 1977–78.

Response to Violence in the Family. 2000 "P" St. N.W., Suite 508, Washington, D.C. 20036.

FILMS

A Family Affair. Written and produced by Susan Shadburne-Wilvinton, narrated by Ed Asner. Color, 16mm, 45 min. Available from Visucom Productions, Inc., Box 5472, Redwood City, Calif. 94063; tel. (415) 363-5566.

No Longer Alone. Produced by Chris LaBeau. Color, 16mm, 30 min. Contact Washington State Shelter Network, 1063 So. Capitol Way, Rm. 217, Olympia, Wash. 98501; tel. (208) 753-4621.

Access to the Future: Serving Disabled Young Women

Katherine Corbett and Merle Froschl
with Jennifer Luna Bregante and Leslie Levy

> *Disabled children have to be able to believe as much as any children in the world that they can continue to live and be happy and functional—that there is a future for them.*[1]

Introduction

In the general population, one in ten Americans has a disability that is physical or emotional in nature.[2] Within this total of approximately 36 million people, disabled women outnumber disabled men.[3] While the vast majority of the disabled population becomes disabled in adulthood, statistics for disabled youth indicate that there are approximately nine million such children between the ages of five and twenty-one in the United States today.[4]

Among disabled youth, it would not be an exaggeration to state that disabled girls and young women are unseen and underserved. The traditional agencies serving youth or serving girls do not, for the most part, consider the disabled population and its needs; and disabled females are disproportionately underrepresented in special education programs serving people with disabilities.

Since October 1980, The Disabled Women's Educational Project, of the Disability Rights Education and Defense Fund, Inc. (D.R.E.D.F.), in Berkeley, California, has been gathering information which documents the inadequacies of services for disabled girls and women, throughout the educational system.[5] One finding of this research, conducted through surveys and through direct experiences with disabled girls and women throughout the country, is that counseling is a significant problem area in the educational experiences and lives of young disabled women. For even when disabled women are given relatively equal education and employment opportunities (which is not very often), advice from counselors tends to keep women in stereotypic roles.

Throughout the years, this pattern has not changed significantly. But with the emergence recently of the disability rights movement, disabled adults are beginning to speak for themselves, and beginning to reevaluate standard counseling issues. This has been a significant factor in the change that has begun to take place.

Nevertheless, as far as the authors are aware, there is little written information for counselors of disabled young women, and the work that has been done in this area is not widely reported outside of the disability rehabilitation community. Since so little work has been done in terms of developing programs for counseling disabled young women, this article cannot provide readily available models to follow. However, sensitive adaptations of other contemporary approaches to counseling young women are possible, inasmuch as the problems of disabled and nondisabled females intersect at many points. A balanced judgment of similarities and differences in the needs of disabled and nondisabled adolescent women depends upon a grasp of issues that are distinct in the lives of the disabled population.

Underlying Stereotypes

The two pervasive attitudes that underly the stereotypes held about people with disabilities are the assumptions that disabled people are inherently either "different than" or "less than" nondisabled people. These attitudes have permeated all the services designed for people with disabilities and have created a discriminatory pattern that results in low educational aspirations, limited access to jobs, and economic deprivation.

In a comprehensive analysis of how America and its schools perceive disabled persons, John Gleidman and William Roth assert that disabled persons are assigned the role of permanent "sick person." Since society does not expect disabled people to fulfill "normal" functions, it limits them to working at "getting better."

While such limited expectations might be permissible for a person with the flu, they are absurd for a group which comprises 10 percent of the children and 20 percent of the adults in this country.[6]

Even the language used to describe persons with disabilities is fraught with negative and dependent connotations: "handicapped" (derived from holding cap in hand, as in begging), "cripple" (derived from "creep"), and "invalid" (meaning not valid), to name only a few. While "disability" is not entirely positive either, it is used here since it is the term most commonly used nationally, and the term used by advocates to self-describe the disability rights movement.

Double and Triple Discrimination

The problems facing disabled people—access barriers, negative attitudes, and low expectations—are further compounded for disabled females by sex-role stereotyping. The severe disadvantage that disabled women suffer is revealed in the economic and social realities which they face. After twelve years of pubic education, disabled women all too often find themselves ill-equipped to do anything but remain in the family home and, ultimately, to be institutionalized.[7] While disabled men and women both face discouraging employment prospects, the prospects for economic self-sufficiency are particularly grim for disabled women. Bureau of Census statistics show the mean earnings for disabled women to be $5,835 as compared to $13,363 for disabled men.[8] Disabled women are almost twice as likely as disabled men to be unemployed. This figure takes on even greater significance in light of the fact that the unemployment rate for disabled males—approximately 35 percent—is one of the highest unemployment rates for any group in the country.[9]

Compared with the economic situation of both nondisabled women and disabled men, the economic realities for disabled women are even worse, and worse still for racial and ethnic minorities within this population. If disabled women face double discrimination, then disabled women of color are triply disadvantaged. Consider the decreasing nature of the following statistics, which can be viewed as an inverted triangle, with white nondisabled males at the top: for every dollar earned by a white nondisabled male, a white disabled male earns 60 cents; a white nondisabled female, 59 cents; a black nondisabled male, 36 cents; a black disabled female, 12 cents.[10] In addition, social class issues are made clear by the statistic that persons with lower family incomes are twice as likely to become disabled as are persons from higher income families.[11]

The realities of this double and triple discrimination affect many areas of counseling disabled young women. While it is not possible to discuss them all in depth, this article raises some of the major issues: role models, education, independence, work, and interpersonal relationships. First, it discusses evidence of sex bias and stereotyping in these areas, and then suggests positive approaches and strategies for change.

Role Models

*I never knew what would happen to me when I
left school. It scared me. I used to believe that when I
graduated I'd die or live with my family forever.
That was because I'd never met a deaf woman.*

This statement, made by a deaf woman recalling her childhood, dramatizes the lack of role models available to disabled women in our society. Rendered completely invisible, a young disabled woman will not see herself reflected in books, movies, or television. Except for a few scattered poster-child images (usually evoking pity) and the larger-than-life stories of Helen Keller, there are few—if any—images of disabled women functioning in society.

The experience of invisibility begins in childhood when, for the most part, disabled children grow up isolated from any adults with disabilities. Nearly all grow up in nondisabled families and neighborhoods, constituting a substrata with neither a unifying identity nor a community. Often special schools or institutions become the disabled child's "community," but even here the staff is most often nondisabled. So, while the child's peers might be all disabled, there are still no positive role models of disabled adults who are independent, working, and feeling good about themselves.

Classroom materials do not provide the disabled child with any positive images. In a recent study, extensive observations and teacher/director interviews in more than one dozen mainstreamed and special education early childhood classrooms in California, North Carolina, Illinois, and New York revealed not one situation inclusive of images of disabled people. Nowhere—in materials or curriculum (with the exception of a very few books)—was there an image of a disabled child or adult functioning in society.[12]

Even when disabled persons are included in children's books, few of the images are positive, and rarely is the disabled person an adult. The portrayal of nondisabled adults continues to be strongly sex stereotyped.[13] Images of disabled people are absent from standard texts,[14] and materials developed for special education classes are often prone to heavy sex-stereotyping.[15] Recently, one young girl in a special education classroom brought home her newest reading book, a book designed to help with learning the alphabet. The final two pages asked, "Would you rather by a young man (Y) and climb a mountain tall . . . or just be a zero (Z) and be nothing much at all?" In the book's illustration, a little girl chalked up the figure of a zero for Z, while a robust young boy on a mountaintop represented Y. The young female student chose to be the Y—what would you choose![16]

This almost total absence of positive images profoundly affects the individual's self-image and self-esteem. Overcoming a negative self-image is a recurrent theme in the lives of young disabled women.[17] And how could it be otherwise? Superficial standards and the media-imposed image of physical attractiveness are unrealistic attainments for all women, but especially for disabled women, whom society views as physically "different." In addition, since female sexual identity in this society is defined largely in terms of physical appearance, disabled women are often dismissed as "asexual."[18]

For disabled women of color, self-image and identity become an even more complicated issue. As Barbara Chin, an Asian disabled woman states: "I'm a member of three minorities: I'm a woman, Asian, and disabled. Which do I identify with most strongly? It's like a triangle. It depends on the circumstances which point of the triangle is on top."[19]

Education

In high school I didn't have a regular math class. I didn't have an algebra or geometry book in braille though I did get braille books, and more individual attention. I loved the sciences but there were no special aids in biology. No models to feel, and the textbook wasn't in braille. I got a "D." In college the teacher let me feel around and probe as much as I wanted in the dissected rats. I got an "A."

Schools follow the rest of society in their assumptions about children with disabilities. The "permanent patient" viewpoint is seen in the disparate academic and social expectations for disabled and nondisabled students. An assumption of inferior capabilities is evident in all areas of the disabled child's educational program, including placement, educational opportunities, and assessment for special education classes. It is in the last-mentioned that sex-role bias and stereotyping become key factors.

Data collected by the Office for Civil Rights, U.S. Department of Education, in the Fall of 1980, reveal that approximately two-thirds of the students identified as in need of specialized educational services were boys, and only one-third were girls. Although there is some variation among the states, these ratios are consistent on the numbers of girls and boys considered in need of special help.

There is no physiological explanation that is sufficient to account for the great disparity in the ratios. Several researchers have identified sex-role stereotyping as an important factor. One author commenting on the finding that males labeled as retarded have higher I.Q.s on average than do females so labeled, wonders: "Could it be that society is able to tolerate a greater amount of subnormality in a woman than in a man? If only the most visibly subnormal females are referred and labeled, this factor could account for our finding that labeled females have lower I.Q. test scores than labeled males."[20] It is among the categories of learning disabled and emotionally disturbed that the greatest differences in identification rates between girls and boys occur—exactly the areas where subjective judgments are most influential.[21]

Sex, race, and ethnicity are all factors in the labeling of children. Studies have found that more white children are labeled superior, fewer retarded, than nonwhite or non-English-speaking children. For boys and minority race children who may be incorrectly "labeled" as in need of special services, identification may burden them with a label they must carry all their lives. Bias in identification, however, may limit the educational opportunities of those disabled women and girls who are, in fact, in need of specialized services but do not receive them.

Independence

When I got my first power wheelchair . . . I felt
like a queen! We went to the grocery store that night
. . . I was just exuberant. To be able to do something
under my own power was wonderful.

As with all young women, the issue of independence for disabled women is critical. Whether it is learning to handle a car or an electric wheelchair, developing increasing independence is a natural rite of passage from youth into adulthood.

The transition to independence, however, may be particularly complicated for young women with disabilities. When negative and extra-protective social attitudes combine with an absence of appropriate role models, young women with disabilities are often inhibited, if not outright prohibited, from seeking physical independence. Without physical independence, disabled young women cannot complete the necessary developmental tasks and economic steps required for adulthood.

Frequently, a combination of negative attitudes and cultural misperceptions prevent independence. For example, many nondisabled people assume that persons with mental retardation will require permanent supervision. Since the great majority of mentally retarded persons are minimally disabled, and blend thoroughly into the nondisabled population once they are out of schools and other institutions, this restrictive projection is inaccurate.

A person's need to become independent is universal. The existence of a disability does not prohibit that desire. The fulfillment of the need, however, does require that imagination and creativity be applied to problems which create special barriers for the disabled.

In this regard, there has been a mushrooming of community-based services to aid the drive toward independent living.[22] These services include community group homes where people can learn necessary skills and then move into the community; outreach services that inform people of new options; independent living skills classes in schools and service centers; and community support groups for people who are making the transition from dependence to independence.

Work

I think I am a good teacher. Even with my handicap, I felt I was better than some teachers with all their faculties. I never doubted my ability.

Unfortunately, few disabled women have an opportunity to find the satisfaction with work expressed in the foregoing lines. Vocational education and training are crucial if disabled women are to make use of their talents and achieve independence. Studies show that at least until 1978, more than two-thirds of the vocational education provided for disabled women consisted of training which was not intended to prepare them to compete on the open job market.[23] Examples cited in one study include older age at time of referral for rehabilitation (34 years for women, 30.7 years for men) and fewer women rehabilitated into wage-earning occupations (97.2 percent of men, 70.4 percent of women in 1977).[24] As with the nondisabled population, disabled women are clustered in a few career areas, mainly service occupations, and disabled men are placed in a far wider range of occupational fields.[25]

Guidance counseling and the development of career/occupational expectations are factors of unknown dimension in the vocational development of disabled young women. It has been found that vocational tracking occurs both on the basis of disability and on the basis of sex. Disabled women tend to receive occupational counseling that channels them into low paying "sit down" professions; i.e., typist, bookkeeper, and speech therapist, rather than encouragement toward other "sit down" but higher paying professions requiring higher education; i.e., computer programmer, scientist, or lawyer.[26]

Although the employment situation for women with disabilities is bleak, many individuals have successfully challenged limiting stereotypes to become workers. It is important that disabled young women are encouraged to see themselves as workers, whether in the home or outside the home; only in this way will they be able to become part of the mainstream.

Interpersonal Relationships

Most people are ignorant and don't know what real love is . . . They don't know how to reach out and touch us because they're afraid we're going to kill them or hurt them or something. They don't know how to say, "Hey, you're a person, too, and I understand you're mentally retarded."

Societal attitudes toward disabled women are perhaps most damaging in the interpersonal areas of forming intimate friendships and establishing independent family ties. Few socially-sanctioned private roles are viewed as appropriate for disabled women and, as noted earlier, relevant role models are virtually invisible. Michelle Fine and Adrienne Asch have reported on the social indicators that point to disabled women's disadvantaged position: "While marriage may not be a preferred status for an increasing number of women, we include it as a customary measure of social options and position. Given this, disabled women are less likely than nondisabled women to be married, are likely to marry later and are more likely to be divorced."[27]

When a disabled woman tries to fulfill the role of mother, she meets incredible resistance. In the past few years, a number of disabled women have been taken to court to prove that they can adequately care for their children. Such actions are often initiated by people completely outside the family unit, such as neighbors. These people cannot imagine how a blind, deaf, retarded, or physically disabled person can possibly care for her children. The result is often a humiliating "show and tell," in which, for example, the disabled mother must diaper the baby in open court, before being allowed to take the child home again.[28]

Positive Strategies

You don't have to have 100 percent of the world
at your disposal. No one does. But what you have can
fill up a whole life. The world is enormous. No one
gets it all.

Despite all the odds, disabled women do develop friendships, finish school, live on their own, get married, and become parents. In themselves, they provide some of the most positive images and role models for disabled young women. While patterns of discrimination against disabled women continue to exist, a great deal has nevertheless been accomplished and changed.

Much of this work has been done by disabled women in the disability rights movement. But there is also a great deal that can be done by people such as counselors—nondisabled or disabled— who work with disabled young women. Following are brief descriptions of strategies for change applicable to this endeavor.

1. Legal Remedies:

There are many laws on the city, state, and federal level that protect disabled people from discrimination. The most used of these are Section 504 of the Rehabilitation Act of 1973 and P.L. 94-142 of the Education Act. The laws are the legal tool of a movement fighting for the civil rights of the disabled population. Section 504 provides general protection against discrimination on the basis of disability. In the area of education, P.L. 94-142 becomes important. P.L. 94-142 requires each state which chooses to receive federal funds to guarantee each disabled child a "free, appropriate public education in the least restrictive environment." For more information, contact your state human rights commission or department of rehabilitation.

2. Advocacy:

Because of widespread barriers, advocacy is often a necessary strategy in order for persons with disabilities to gain basic access to "public" places and to obtain the rights to which they are entitled. During the school years, parents of disabled children often assume this task. Such advocacy is crucial to disabled children and youths. The long-range goal, however, is self-advocacy, without which the disabled person is always dependent on the availability of another person for help. Thus, as disabled youths grow older, it is important for them to learn how to assume more responsibility for furthering their own rights.

Advocacy can take many forms, from writing petitions for accessible public transportation, to organizing the community to demand adequate seating for wheelchairs in movies and theatres, to gathering information on laws protecting persons from discrimination. Many cities have active parents' groups which can train parents as advocates. If the child is a ward of the state, or the parents cannot be located, or the parents give permission, the state must, by law, appoint someone to guard the child's educational rights. This is the "surrogate parent" section of P.L. 94-142. The authority of this person is limited to acting as an advocate for the child's educational needs.

Even within community facilities and state institutions, the child has a right to an independent advocate. This person cannot be an employee of the institution responsible for the child's education. While there is much in the law that remains unclarified (for example it is not known whether the surrogate is entitled to be paid for the services, or to be provided with adequate training), it is clear that any legal costs involved in negotiating for the child's educational rights will be borne by the state.

3. INFORMATION AND RESOURCES:

In order to counsel effectively and to become an advocate, it is essential to become informed about various disabilities, about laws, and about disability-related issues, such as adequate equipment, accessibility, and services. Counselors need information about the accessibility of vocational programs; about disabled student programs on campuses; about accessible housing and transportation; and about the availability of large print or braille editions of materials and other necessary aids.

It is often difficult, however, to locate the information which may be wanted. If you don't know where to start, there are several national networks with offices in every state: 1) The Governor's Committee on Employment of the Handicapped, 2) The State Council on the Handicapped, and 3) State Protection and Advocacy. In addition, Independent Living Projects, located in every state, have information on housing, disability-related equipment, advocacy, work, transportation, and services. Ultimately, your best resources will be the ones in your own community.

In the Bibliography you will find a list of additional resources that should prove helpful in gathering information. *No More Stares*, a book developed by D.R.E.D.F., is particularly useful, providing a comprehensive bibliography of resources. In addition, it offers both a frank discussion of the problems of growing up female and disabled and a wide, documented range of possible role models.

4. CHANGING ATTITUDES—OUR OWN AND OTHERS:

One of the most common pitfalls for a counselor who is beginning to work with disabled young women is to assume that you know ":what she needs"; another pitfall is to rely on a nondisabled professional to tell you. It is important to realize that the disabled person herself is in the best position to tell you her needs. If she needs help, the best resource will be an independent living center or another disabled adult in the community. There is no better "expert" than another person with a disability.

Because there has been so little information generally available about persons with disabilities, there have been limited opportunities for the nondisabled population to learn about the needs of persons with disabilities. Further, a great deal of misinformation has been passed along. By far the best way to learn about disabilities is to spend time with disabled persons. Direct association with a new group is not only the quickest avenue to reliable information, but has the most lasting impact on the initiate.

Another way to counteract the lack of information, as well as the misinformation, about disabled people is through an examination of one's own attitudes and assumptions. At present, a consciousness-raising packet is being developed by the "Women and Disability Awareness Project," a group of disabled and nondisabled women who have met to discuss disabled women, feminism, and the links between the disability rights and women's movements. The purpose of the packet is to raise awareness about how women as a group and disabled people as a group are affected by similar processes of bias, stereotyping, and discrimination. Through the use of consciousness-raising, a uniquely feminist format, it is hoped that a forum will be provided for mutual self-discovery, sharing of personal experience, and exploration of possibilities for change. (See Bibliography.)

It is important, of course, to begin to change attitudes as early as possible. Mainstreaming—the integration of disabled and nondisabled children in classrooms—affords the opportunity to break down damaging stereotypes at an early age. While educational programs were planned to help disabled children adjust to mainstreamed classrooms, it was soon discovered that it would be necessary to help nondisabled children shape—or reshape—their attitudes, if mainstreaming was to be a success. Since the enactment of the Education for All Handicapped Children Act of 1975, several projects have been developed to work toward this goal.[29]

5. ROLE MODELS:

It is important to foster all possible contacts between disabled youth and disabled adults. One effective and relatively easy way to facilitate this is to set up "peer groups" for disabled girls and women in your community. These groups can be comprised of disabled young women who are approximately the same age, but with different kinds of disabilities, or of females with the same disability, but who are of different ages. Being female and disabled will be the common bond. This peer structure allows the participants to realize that they are not alone in their concerns and problems. It also encourages members to help one another, thereby enhancing leadership skills and developing community resources. Since disabled young women have lacked role models, especially of adults, a good way to provide such models is for a disabled adult to lead or facilitate the group, or to share these tasks with a nondisabled group leader.

This past year, through the Disabled Women's Educational Project, D.R.E.D.F. has organized peer group meetings with disabled young women in various regions throughout the country. These groups, which have met in a retreat-like atmosphere over a weekend, have taken place in Berkeley, California; Pocatello, Idaho; Minneapolis, Minnesota; and Eugene, Oregon.

Another approach is to provide role models through your own agency or institution by hiring disabled women, not only to work with disabled youth, but in all facets of the program. It may be necessary to investigate policies or attitudes that prohibit disabled women from participating, and then petition to have these discriminatory practices changed. If you do not currently have disabled people working in your agency, in all likelihood it means that some part of your agency is screening them out. Factors to consider are: personnel policies that require "normal" abilities; medical tests that automatically disqualify all disabled applicants for employment; attitudes such as, "that kind of person would disrupt work here"; inaccessible work place or bathrooms.

If disabled people can't get jobs, then they can't be available as role models for disabled girls and women. Each one of us is in a position to begin to make change in this area.

Conclusion

An underlying theme throughout this article has been that of the similarities and differences between the needs of disabled and nondisabled young women. In order to help disabled young women not to personalize the rejection they experience, it is important to acknowledge that there is specific and ongoing stereotyping and discrimination practiced against those persons who are perceived as having a disability. Disabled young women need to realize that societal attitudes, not their own individual failings, are at the root of the problem.

However, it is also important to recognize the parallel concerns that connect disabled and nondisabled women's lives. While disabled women may have to struggle more openly with physical and attitudinal barriers, the issues—society's narrow definition of sexuality, "appropriate" independence for women, the need for meaningful work—are the same. It is possible that the struggle of disabled women will help to redefine the issues for all women.

NOTES

1.   This quotation, and all the quotations cited throughout the article, are taken from *No More Stares*, a role model book published by The Disability Right Education and Defense Fund, Inc., Berkeley, California, 1982. (See Bibliography.)

2. John Gleidman and William Roth, *The Unexpected Minority: Handicapped Children in America* (New York: Harcourt Brace Jovanovich, 1980), p. 503.

The legal definition of a disabled person, taken from Section 843.J of the Federal Register Final Regulations to Implement Section 504 of the Rehabilitation Act of 1973 reads as follows:

> "Handicapped person" means any person who (i) has a physical or mental impairment which substantially limits one or more major life activities, (ii) has a record of such an impairment, or (iii) is regarded as having such an impairment. . . ."

3. Rehab Group, *The Digest of Data on Persons with Disabilities* (Washington, D.C.: The Group, 1979).

4. Gleidman and Roth, *The Unexpected Minority,* p. 6.

5. The Disabled Women's Educational Project is funded under a grant from the Women's Educationals Equity Act Program, United States Department of Education, which was the first and is still one of the only agencies that has made a commitment to funding programs dealing with issues of women and disability.

6. Gleidman and Roth, *The Unexpected Minority,* p. 41.

7. *Concerns*, no. 9 (June 1983), Council of Chief State School Officers, Resource Center on Sex Equity, Washington, D.C., p. 1.

8. United States Department of Health, Education, and Welfare, Steering Committee on Women's Issues and Women's Action Program, "Sex Discrimination in H.E.W.: An Agenda for Action," March 11, 1980, and S. Levitan and R. Taggot, *Jobs for the Disabled* (Baltimore: Johns Hopkins University Press, 1977), p. 9, as reported in *Concerns*.

9. Bureau of the Census data from March 1982, as reported in *Concerns*.

10. "Employment Problems of Disabled Persons," *Monthly Labor Review*, March, 1977, as reported in Council on Interracial Books for Children *Bulletin*, vol 8, nos. 6, 7, 1977, pp 20–21; and Mark F. Odintz with Deborah Ellis, "Disability, Sex, and Race Issues in Educational Equity: A Review of Current Literature" (Disability Rights Education and Defense Fund, Inc., 1982).

11. Gleidman and Roth, *The Unexpected Minority,* p. 5.

12. Reported in Barbara Sprung, "Introduction," *Creating a New Mainstream: An Early Childhood Training Manual for an 'Inclusionary' Curriculum,* 1982. Unpublished manuscript.

13. Nancy Gropper and Amy Shuster, "Separate Is Not Equal: Intended and Implicit Messages about the Disabled in Children's Literature," *Equal Play,* vol. 2, nos. 1, 2 (Winter–Spring, 1981), pp. 5–7.

14. Emily Strauss Watson, "Handicapism in Children's Books: A Five-Year Update," *Bulletin,* vol. 13, nos. 4, 5, 1982, pp. 3–5, as reported in *Concerns.*

15. Patricia Gillespie and Alan Fink, "The Influence of Sexism on the Education of Handicapped Children," *Exceptional Children,* vol. 41, no. 3 (November 1974), pp. 155–162.

16. As reported in *Concerns,* p. 2.

17. Carrillo *et al., No More Stares;* and Fine and Asch, "Disabled Women: Sexism without the Pedestal," *Journal of Sociology and Social Welfare,* vol. 8, no. 2 (July 1981), pp. 233–248.

18. Yvonne Duffy, *All Things Are Possible* (Ann Arbor, Mich.: A.J. Garvin Associates, 1981), *passim.*

19. Carrillo *et al., No More Stares,* p. 8.

20. J. Mercer, *Labeling the Mentally Retarded* (Berkeley, Ca.: University of California Press, 1973).

21. As reported in *Concerns,* p. 2.

22. Every state has independent living centers. Call the office of your state's department of rehabilitation for information.

23. J. Corbett O'Toole and Cece Weeks, "What Happens After School? A Study of Disabled Women and Education," Far West Laboratory, San Francisco, 1978.

24. *Ibid.*

25. *Ibid.*

26. Katherine Corbett, Susanne Lea, and Jane Sprague Zones, "Equity Issues in Special Education," Disability Rights Education and Defense Fund, Inc., 1981.

27. Fine and Asch, "Disabled Women: Sexism without the Pedestal."

28. J. Corbett O'Toole, "Disabled Women: The Case of the Missing Role Model," *Independent*, no. 2 (1979), pp. 12–16.

29. The Kids Project, a puppet education program designed to teach children about a variety of disabilities: The Kids Project, N.Y.S. Office of Mental Retardation and Developmental Disabilities, 4 Holland Ave., Albany, NY 12229; The KIDS Project, Inc., Keys to Introducing Disability in Society: Whittier School, 1645 Milvia St., Berkeley, CA 94709; R.A.P.S. (Resource Access Projects), training and technical assistance for the Head Start mainstreaming effort: Administration for Children, Youth and Families, Head Start Bureau, Washington, D.C. 20024.

Bibliography*

EQUITY ISSUES IN SPECIAL EDUCATION

Campbell, Patricia B., "Diagnosing the Problem: Sex Stereotyping in Special Education," (materials developed under the Women's Educational Equity Act Program, U.S. Department of Education, printed and distributed by Education Development Center, 55 Chapel Street, Newton, Massachusetts 02160).

Corbett, K., Lea, Susanne, and Zones, Jane Sprague, "Equity Issues in Special Education," Disability Rights Education and Defense Fund, Inc., 1981.

Council of Chief State School Officers Resource Center on Sex Equity, *Concerns*, Issue IX, June 1983. (400 North Capitol Street, N.W., Suite 379, Washington, D.C. 20001).

Danek, Marita, Wax, Teena M., "Deaf Women and Double Jeopardy: Challenge for Research and Practice," Gallaudet College.

Gillespie, P. and Fink, A., "The Influence of Sexism on the Education of Handicapped Children," *Exceptional Children*, Vol. 41, No. 3, November 1974.

Greenberg, Jill Moss, "The Bias Trap: The Interaction of Handicapism and Other Forms of Bias," *Newflash*, Vol. 3, No. 4, 1981.

Odintz, Mark with Ellis, Deborah, "Disability, Sex, and Race Issues in Educational Equity: A Review of Current Literature," Disability Rights Education and Defense Fund, Inc., 1982.

SEX BIAS IN IDENTIFICATION/EVALUATION

Bernknopf, Linda A., "Responses of Adolescents on a Masculinity-Femininity Scale and a Stereotyping Questionnaire," *Exceptional Children*, Vol. 47, No. 1, September 1980.

*This bibliography is adapted from *Concerns* no. 9 (June 1983).

Broverman, I. K., *et al.*, "Sex Role Stereotyping and Clinical Judgements of Mental Health," *Journal of Consulting and Clinical Psychology*, 34, January 1970.

Caplan, Paula J. and Kinsbourne, "Sex Differences in Response to School Failure," *Journal of Learning Disabilities*, Vol. 7, No. 4, April 1974.

Caplan, Paula J., "Sex, Age, Behavior, and School Subject as Determinants of Report of Learning Problems," *Journal of Learning Disabilities*, Vol. 10, No. 5, May 1977.

Emery, E. Joan, "The Effects of Sexism on the Classification of Children With Learning Disabilities," *Journal of School Psychology*, 1973.

Gillespie-Silver and Heshusius, Lous, "Mental Retardation: A Double Standard for the Sexes," *Equal Play*, Winter/Spring 1981.

Gregory, M. K., "Sex Bias in School Referrals," *Journal of School Psychology*, Vol. 15, No. 1, 1977.

Gross, Alice D., "Cultural Influences on Sex Ratios in Learning Disabilities," paper presented at the World Congress on Future Special Education at Stering, Scotland, June 1978, reprinted in HEW:ERIC.

Hagin, Rosa, "Longitudinal Study of Learning Disabled Students," *The Observer, A Digest of Learning*, Vol. 1, No. 4, December 1980.

Leinhardt, Gaea, *et al.*, "Sex and Race Differences in Learning Disabilities Classrooms," paper presented at the Annual Meeting of the American Educational Research Association, April 1981, reprinted in HEW:ERIC.

Mercer, J., *Labeling the Mentally Retarded*, Berkeley, University of California Press, 1973.

Mumpower, D. L., "Sex Ratios Found in Various Types of Referred Exceptional Children," *Exceptional Children*, 1970.

Phipps, P., "An Examination of Teacher Perceptions of Boys and Girls With School Learning and·Behavior Problems," Ph.D. dissertation, University of California, 1977.

Quantz, Richard A., "Sex Bias and the Social Function of Mild Mental Retardation," *Journal of Educational Equity and Leadership*, Vol. 2, No. 3, Spring 1982.

Reschly, Daniel J. and Jipson, Frederick J., "Ethnicity, Geographic Local, Age, Sex, and Urban-Rural Residence as Variables in the Prevalence of Mild Retardation," *American Journal of Mental Deficiency*, 1976.

Singer, Benjamin D. and Osborn, Richard W., "Social Clas and Sex Differences in Admission Patterns of the Mentally Retarded," *American Journal of Mental Deficiency*, 1970.

Smith, I. Leon and Greenberg, Sandra, "Teacher Attitudes and the Labelling Process," *Exceptional Children*, February 1975.

Spaulding, Robert, "Achieving, Creativity, and Self-Concept Correlates of Teacher-Pupil Transactions in Elementary School," U.S. Department of Health, Education, and Welfare, Office of Education, Cooperative Research Project No. 1352, 1963.

Tudor, William, Tudor, Jeanette, and Gore, Walter, R.. "The Effect of Sex Role Differences on the Societal Reaction to Mental Retardation," *Social Forces*, Vol. 57, No. 3, March 1979.

Warren, Sue Allen and Gardner, David C., "Correlates of Class Rank of High School Handicapped Students in Mainstream Vocational Education Programs," *Adolescence*, Vol. XVI, No. 62, Summer 1981.

BIAS IN CURRICULUM AND TEXTBOOKS

Equal Play, Vol. II, Nos. 1 and 2, Nonsexist Child Development Project, Women's Action Alliance, Inc., 1981.

Interracial Books for Children Bulletin, Vol. 8, Nos. 6 and 7, 1977 and Vol. 13, Nos. 4 and 5, 1982.

McCloud, B., Mitchell, M. and Tagland, G., "Content Analysis of Basal Reading Texts for Normal and Retarded Children," *Journal of Special Education*, Vol. 10, No. 3, 1976.

VOCATIONAL AND POSTSECONDARY OPPORTUNITIES FOR DISABLED STUDENTS

Bliss, Mary and Schwartz, Adele, *Exploring Attitudes Toward Women With Disabilities: A Curriculum Guide for Employers and Educators*, New York City Commission on the Status of Women, 1980.

Cegelka, P., "Sex Role Stereotyping in Special Education: A Look at Secondary Work-Study Programs," *Exceptional Children*, Vol. 42, No. 6, March 1976.

Cook, L., and Rossett, A., "The Sex Role Attitudes of Deaf Adolescent Women and Their Implications for Vocational Choice," *American Annals of the Deaf*, 1975.

Danker-Brown, P. Sigelman, C., and Flexer, R., "Sex Bias in Vocational Programming for Handicapped Students," *Journal of Special Education*, Vol. 12, No. 4, Winter 1978.

Danek, Marita, M., and White, Francine, "Expanding Occupational Choices for Deaf Women," Gallaudet College, 1982, counseling materials.

Dodd, Judy E., "Overcoming Occupational Stereotypes Related to Sex and Deafness," *American Annals of the Deaf*, 1977.

Levitan, S. and Taggert R., *Jobs for the Disabled*, The Johns Hopkins University Press, 1977.

Lombana, Judy H., "Facilitating Guidance of Deaf Students: Challenges and Opportunities for Counselors," *The Vocational Guidance Quarterly*, Vol. 27, No. 4, 1979.

Moccia, Lianne, "Occupational Stereotyping by High School Deaf Students: A Preliminary Survey," 1981.

The National Easter Seal Society, *Rehabilitation Literature*, Special Issue Devoted to Women, Vol. 43, No. 7-8, July–August 1982.

Scheffelin, Margaret A.M., "Employability of Persons Who are Both Deaf and Blind," 1980, available from author upon request.

U.S. Department of Health, Education, and Welfare, Steering Committee on Women's Issues and the Women's Action Program, *Sex Discrimination in the Department of Health, Education, and Welfare: An Agenda for Action*, March 11, 1980.

DISABLED WOMEN IN SOCIETY

Barnartl, Sharon N., "The Socio-Economic Status of Deaf Women: Are They Doubly Disadvantaged?", Gallaudet College, unpublished.

Campling, Jo, editor, *Images of Ourselves—Women With Disabilities Talking,* Routledge and Kegan Paul Ltd., Boston, Massachusetts, 1981.

Carrillo, A., Corbett, K., and Lewis, V., *No More Stares*, Disability Rights Education and Defense Fund, Inc. (2032 San Pablo Ave., Berkeley, CA 94703), 1982.

Chaussy, Annette, "Deaf Women and the Women's Movement," *The Deaf American*, April 1977.

Corbett, K. and Weeks, Ce Ce, *What Happens After School? A Study of Disabled Women and Education*, Far West Laboratory for Women's Educational Equity Communications Network, San Francisco, 1978.

Fine, Michelle and Asch, Adrienne, "Disabled Women: Sexism Without the Pedestal," *Journal of Sociology and Social Welfare*, Vol. VIII, No. 2, July 1981.

Maryland Commission for Women, "Disabled Women: A Growing Force," *Maryland Women*, Summer 1982.

Off Our Backs, Special Issue on Women and Disability, Vol. XI, No. 5, May 1981.

Women and Disability Awareness Project, Educational Equity Concepts, Inc., 440 Park Avenue South, New York, N.Y. 10016.

Zabolai-Csekme, Era, "Women and Disability, Kit No. 1," JUNIC/NGO
    Services on Women and Development, 1981, copies and information
    available from Development Education Centre, UNICEF Office for
    Europe, Palais des Nations, CH-1211 Geneva 10.

About the Contributors

Jennifer Luna Bregante has worked for a decade in both family therapy and psychodrama. Currently, she also has a private consulting business in the San Francisco Bay area. She has three disabled children, the youngest of whom has recently graduated from high school. Bregante has been active in the movement to provide services for disabled youth in community facilities, and has been closely associated with the work of Youth Advocates, San Francisco.

Teresa Contreras, a volunteer counselor and board member of the East Los Angeles Rape Hotline since 1976, became its director in 1982. Born and reared in the barrio of South Tucson, Arizona, she holds a bachelor of science degree in behavioral science from Pacific Union College, Angwin, California. She has worked in East Los Angeles over the past ten years in the areas of family planning, cancer education, child abuse, and sexual assault.

Katherine Corbett is coordinator of the Disabled Women's Educational Equity Project of the Disability Rights Education and Defense Fund, Berkeley, California. The project is a national undertaking to assess the educational experiences of disabled females, document areas of inequity, and develop remediating materials and strategies. Trained in special education, Corbett has been a classroom teacher of special needs students from the pre-school through the young adult level. She is a co-author of *No More Stares* (1982).

Sue Davidson, information director for New Directions for Young Women, Tucson, is a resident of Seattle. Formerly an editor for The Feminist Press, she also served as a co-director of its high school series, *Women's Lives/Women's Work*. She is co-editor of *The Maimie Papers* (1977), the letters of an early twentieth-century prostitute who became a benefactor for young women of the streets, and editor of *Justice for Young Women: Close-up on Critical Issues* (1982). She received the M.A. in humanities from the University of Chicago.

Merle Froschl is the co-founder and co-director of Educational Equity Concepts, Inc., New York, a nonprofit organization created to develop programs and materials free of sexism, racism, and bias against disability. She is the former director of the Non-Sexist Child Development Project of the Women's Action Alliance, where she initiated and directed Project R.E.E.D. (Resources on Educational Equity for the Disabled) and numerous other programs. She served as field testing coordinator and a co-director of The Feminist Press's *Women's Lives/Women's Work* series.

Lewayne D. Gilchrist is a research scientist at the University of Washington Child Development and Mental Retardation Center, and was formerly a clinician in the university's Department of Psychiatry and Behavioral Sciences. Her research interests are the health and social welfare of adolescents; she has also taught at the elementary through graduate school levels. With Steven Schinke, she has recently completed *Life Skills Counseling with Adolescents* (in press). She received her doctoral degree in social welfare from the University of Washington.

Leslie Levy is an attorney in private practice in Oakland, California. In addition to her interest in issues affecting disabled youth, she has been active in the feminist movement and in the movement for lesbian rights.

Deborah Lodish, M.S.W., is a clinical researcher at the Child Development and Mental Retardation Center, University of Washington, and a clinical social worker at Family Services of King County, specializing in individual, marital, and family therapy. Her work experience has been in health promotion with older adults; group interpersonal skills instruction with adults, adolescents, and children; and counseling with families at the Women's and Children's Clinic, Harborview Medical Center, University of Washington.

Irene D. Mendez is a co-founder of the East Los Angeles Rape Hotline and a present member of its board of directors. Her work experience has included community organizing and service in programs for juvenile diversion and delinquency prevention. A former director of the Eastside Multi-Service Center, Los Angeles, she is currently employee relations representative with the Los Angeles County Department of Community Development. Mendez took her bachelor's degree in psychology/sociology at the University of Texas, El Paso.

Ginny NiCarthy, M.S.W., has led groups for abused women since 1976 and has conducted workshops on a variety of women's issues in the United States and Great Britain. She founded and served as director of the Abused Women's Network, Seattle, and is a past director of Seattle Rape Relief. Currently a counselor in private practice, she is the author of *Assertion Skills for Young Women: A Manual* (1981) and *Getting Free: A Handbook for Women in Abusive Relationships* (1982).

Sue Sapperstein, M.F.C.C., is the founder of Women's Family Services, San Francisco, a clinical and training project committed to the advancement of work in the field of women and girl's psychology. She has led workshops nationally on issues of importance to female youth, including childhood sexual abuse and lesbian adolescence. An activist on behalf of gay youth and gay parent rights, and a lesbian mother, Sapperstein was among the founders of the Sexual Minority Youth Services Coalition, San Francisco.

Steven Paul Schinke is an associate professor of social work at the University of Washington and chairman of social work research at the university's Child Development and Mental Retardation Center. He and his research group are examining models of primary prevention applied to a variety of emotional, social, and health problems among children and adults. Schinke took the Ph.D. in social work at the University of Wisconsin, Madison. He is the editor of *Behavioral Methods in Social Welfare* (1981).

Elaine D. Schroeder is a psychotherapist and consultant in Juneau, Alaska, where she is also coordinator of the sexual assault program of A.W.A.R.E. (Aiding Women from Abuse and Rape Emergencies). A co-founder of Seattle Rape Relief, Schroeder is currently developing expanded counseling approaches for incest survivors. Her activities also include training of social service providers and institutional personnel to work with youth in crisis. She holds a Ph.D. in social welfare from the University of Washington.

Susan Staab, M.S.W., is a clinical researcher at the Child Development and Mental Retardation Center, University of Washington. Her clinical experience has included social work practice in nursing homes, home health care, and mental health. She has participated in promotion of coping skills for school-age mothers and smoking prevention programs with adolescents. Her current research interests are health promotion and assertiveness training in the workplace.

185

New Directions for Young Women is a nonprofit, tax-exempt agency founded in Tucson, Arizona, in 1976. Through direct services and advocacy, New Directions strives to promote the interests of young women affected by the juvenile justice, social service, and educational systems. In every aspect of our work, we examine the impact of sex-role stereotyping and discrimination, and attempt to bring about positive changes in attitudes and institutions. We take an active and vocal role in public forums, sponsor regional conferences and training workshops, and participate in coalitions formed to improve the position of women and youth. To further awareness of the conditions of young women, New Directions has also developed and published a variety of educational materials.

For more information on our programs and publications, contact:

New Directions for Young Women
738 N. 5th Avenue
Tucson, Arizona 85705
(602) 623-3677